MW00929521

Kessler

Once An Insider, Now Without A Church Home

Once An Insider, Now Without A Church Home

One Couple's Faith Crisis Due to the Infiltration and Spread of Authoritarianism, Calvinism, Complementarianism, and Covenants in the Am Evangelical Church

Amanda Farmer

Book Title Copyright © 2018 by Amanda Farmer. All Rights Reserved.

All rights reserved. No part of this book may be reproduced in any form or by any electronic or mechanical means including information storage and retrieval systems, without permission in writing from the author. The only exception is by a reviewer, who may quote short excerpts in a review.

Cover designed by Amanda Farmer, Photography by Gordon Farmer

This book expresses the views solely of the author and do not necessarily reflect the views of the publisher, and the publisher hereby disclaims any responsibility for them.

Amanda Farmer
Visit my website at www.calvinism-faith-crisis.com

Printed in the United States of America

First Printing: October 2018
Farmer Memoirs

ISBN 9781726710916

When we capitulate to evil in the name of "peace," we become the evil. When we suppress truth in the name of "love," we become the lie. When we excuse abuse in the name of "unity," we become the abuser.

—JIM WRIGHT

Table of Contents

Foreword by a Member of Our Small Group

What we know is what we have been taught; rarely do we question the truth of it. We were taught by men and women whom we trusted and respected, so their teaching became our truth, the lens through which we view all of life. Everything that aligns with our truth is accepted and all that is contrary to our truth is declared false.

When we encounter opposition to our truth, we often respond by digging in our heels and declaring that our truth is the only truth, refusing to consider that what we have been taught and used as the foundation for building our life, may indeed be false. We want to be right, so we will deliberately close our minds to considering another understanding of truth. We do not want to admit we were wrong. How devastating it would be to find, halfway through your life, that what you had thought and taught was actually a lie. So you fight hard against any and all who would shake the foundation of what you believe.

This is especially true in churches and with church leaders. The truth becomes distorted and then taught to the next generation, who pass it to the next and the next, until it became a dogma to rally around: "We have the truth and anyone who disagrees with us is guilty of heresy." Using shame and blame and guilt, leaders and teachers convince those within their domain to abandon their own truth and take on the only "real" truth. There is nothing malicious in this coercion, the leaders and teachers are truly convinced that their way is the only way and they genuinely believe they are helping people to find the only real truth. Sadly, far too many people view pastors and teachers as having received special knowledge from God that they, on their own, cannot access. Rather than emulating the early Christians in Berea by searching the Scriptures daily to see if these things were true, congregations tend to rely on a man to tell them what is true instead of allowing the Holy Spirit to make the truth clear.

And that is when problems develop. Pastors quote other pastors and align their teaching with the teachings of other men and staying true to those teachings becomes more important than finding and adhering to God's truth. And then the people suffer.

One evening, Gordon had been unusually quiet during the Bible study portion of our small group meeting. As we started sharing our spiritual needs prior to praying, it was obvious something was greatly troubling him. Finally, he blurted out, "I don't think I'm saved. I don't think I am one God's chosen." The group was stunned into silence.

Most of the group knew that Gordon and Amanda were struggling with teachings from the pastor and associate pastor of our church, but only a few of us understood that the issue was Calvinism. In fact, most of the group wasn't even sure what Calvinism was all about. But it was obvious to all of us that Gordon and Amanda had been deeply hurt by this teaching that had become obvious in the sermons and teachings of our pastor and his associate.

Our Life Group rallied around Gordon and Amanda, encouraging them and affirming their faith at every opportunity. But it had shaken us. Most of the members of our Life Group had known each other since childhood, we had been part of planting our church, and we had chosen to affiliate our church with a denomination that encouraged its people to search the scriptures in their entirety rather than build doctrines on a verse here and a verse there, to seek unity by affirming belief in basic truths and being tolerant of differences of opinion on lesser doctrinal issues. We had been known in the community as a place to go to be accepted and loved regardless of background or life circumstances. For many people who had been betrayed, abandoned or rejected by their biological families, the church people had become a replacement family where love and acceptance abounded. Gordon and Amanda certainly had found that to be true, so had I.

Over the course of the next weeks and months, our group looked at Calvinism and Arminianism and decided that what we believed did not align with either teaching. As one of our group members succinctly said, "I believe in Jesus and what he taught. I don't need anyone telling me what Jesus supposedly meant." But our eyes had been opened and we could not go back to naively listening to our pastors and not hearing the Calvinistic bias in everything they taught. This created a conundrum for all of us. What we had planted nearly 3 decades earlier was turning, mutating into something else. And we felt angry and helpless. How could we stop this slide into Calvinism and away from the love of Jesus?

Looking back, we could see how small changes over the years had accumulated to bring the church to this point. But hindsight could not tell us how to reverse the changes. So we prayed and talked and prayed some more. Week after week after week.

But we became increasingly frustrated with our church leadership, especially the pastor, who seemed totally unconcerned that his teachings were causing a spiritual crisis. When life group members took their concerns over the situation to either the pastor or his associate, the response was that Gordon and Amanda had spiritual issues, probably rooted in their past, that they needed to work through. We were also warned against divisiveness and told that we need to trust our pastors and follow their leading. But why would we follow leaders who were heading down the wrong path?

For Gordon and Amanda, being rejected by the pastors and elders in such a manner left them with a feeling of humiliation and shame, even though they had done nothing wrong. It was hard for them to deal with people who asked them about the situation. They certainly did not want to publicly criticize the pastors, but it was hard not to seek vindication for pursuing the truth.

In our small group, we opted to continue as we had in the past, searching the whole of Scripture for our answers rather than looking to the commentaries by men. But what about church? Did we continue attending a church where the pastors were teaching doctrines and dogmas that did not align with what we believed the Scriptures clearly taught? Did we go looking for another church where Calvinism was not taught? We talked about going to the pastors as a group with our concerns, but eventually ruled that out as we realized that would just get us branded as troublemakers seeking to divide the church, which was not our goal. The pastors had made it clear where they stood and that they would not listen to arguments against their stance. We did not want to walk away from our church family and the relationships we had enjoyed for years, decades for most of us. We felt frustrated and helpless, there simply did not appear to be a way to return to what was taught and believed when we started the church. Some of us checked out other churches in the area but discovered that nearly all of the evangelical churches were also on that slippery slope into Calvinism. Suddenly, the church that had meant home and belonging for us was no longer a place to feel loved and accepted.

Where to go and what to do? The question extended beyond our small group. Some church families just quietly quit coming to church, citing doctrinal differences when asked the reason. Others just attended sporadically, not comfortable with the teaching but not knowledgeable about Calvinism and so unable to cite a reason. Our small group continues to meet, and we pray for the pastors continually.

But the question remains: how do churches get to the point of harming their members? Research shows that it is happening all across the country. Amanda has written out an incredibly honest and accurate account of how our church changed over time from being Spirit led to being governed by the tenets of Calvinism. My prayer is that her retelling of this intensely painful period will alert others in time to prevent their church from heading the same direction.

Introduction From the Author

I have always considered myself to be a Bible-believing evangelical Christian. So what has happened that I have begun to question everything that I have ever believed? This is a story of the journey of my husband and I in a Bible-believing church and how we went from being insiders to being on the outside looking in.

Our general faith world has become saturated with men and movements, all shouting that they have the best "Bible-based" fad to be followed. In our personal world, it was the New Calvinism and the much subtler accentuates of authoritarianism, complementarianism, and covenants that seem to go along with Neo-Calvinism's infiltration. It is a story of what is happening in the Evangelical Free Church of America as well as many of the other independent churches that are springing up in our day. My hope is to encourage people to look more closely at the church that they are involved in and to be aware of what is happening – to ask some questions of the trends around them. Is my church really following the Bible? Or have the latest fads of the day been creeping in? I am not a Greek interpreting scholar but a simple reader of the Word. Therefore, my story does not contain divinity school exogenesis of the scriptures but a layman's understanding of the reading of God's word.

I have changed the names of all those involved in our story to protect the dignity of all participants. None of us is innocent and all need forgiveness for the sin-influenced actions presented here. Names of cities have been changed to provide anonymity also. As with any personal story or memoir, I have made the utmost attempt to write with veracity using church documents, public documents, and personal communications. Our memories are fickle things and therefore, I acknowledge that the memories of others may not completely correlate with my own. I also acknowledge that I cannot know the ultimate motivations of others. I can only speculate from their actions. I am sure that most pastors do not go into the ministry with the motivation of harming others spiritually. They simply get caught up in the sinfulness of us all and lose sight of or are deceived about what the caring of a shepherd should look like in the church of Jesus Christ.

Chapter 1 Two Lives United

I t all begins in 1990. I am a 32-year-old unmarried conservative Mennonite lady. Just a year earlier, I found a cozy two-bedroom ranch home with no basement nestled on a cul-de-sac in Sun Prairie, Minnesota. I fell in love with it and settled in for life as a spinster as by now, I understand that due to the position of my family in the Mennonite church, no Mennonite man will ever choose to marry me. But I am restless and still dream of having a family.

One evening, after returning from a recent adventure with Mercy Ships, I jokingly tell my roommate that I am going to someday place an ad in the personals column of the Superior regional newspaper just to see what kind of replies I get. I have been reading the personals fairly regularly over the last few months, picking out ads of interest and then throwing them away after a couple of weeks. She laughs and encourages me to go for it. And thus, in late March of 1990, I place an ad.

32-year-old NBM SWF looking for companionship and/or someone to share some good times with. This person must be a single widower or a NBM SWM between 28–38 years of age who values Christianity and uses it as a basis for his morality. Must also have a good sense of humor and be able to relax enough to enjoy life. I am independent, adventuresome, and love the outdoors. I enjoy most any outdoor activity, but biking and hiking are my favorites. Looking for someone who is open, honest, caring, and able to accept others the way they are.

I pull out a large envelope from my post office box a few weeks later. The return address is that of *Superior News*. I eagerly rip it open. Inside are nine letters from different men all addressed to Post Office Box 25. I like that this process is blinded; none of the men know who I am. I can answer any of them I want or ignore them all if I so choose. I settle into my recliner when I get home to read. I eliminate several on the first reading—he smokes, he's older than thirty-eight, he's divorced.

I finally pick out three letters that seem to provide possible candidates. But I am particularly drawn to one letter. The man presents himself in a straightforward, honest, unassuming manner.

Hello, I have been reading your ad ever since it came out. I still don't know that writing you is right. You seem to have a very specific person in mind and I don't know if I am inside your parameters or not. I do enjoy the outdoors; biking and hiking are great fun. I have never been married and am a white male, age 34. I am a Christian (Lutheran) and enjoy my involvement in the church. I am a member of my church's council and attend services regularly. I think I am caring, and honest and other people seem to think so too. I like to think I can take people for what they are. Yet, I think that is probably something others have to judge in me or you. It's not something a person can judge about themselves. So far so good. Perhaps! Now for the part that has me stumped. If you ask anyone if I know how to relax enough to enjoy life, they would probably say that I don't, and I guess they would probably be right. I need someone to help me relax and not take things so seriously. Just a little about myself. (If you are still reading.) I am 6'4" tall, slim looking even at 220 lbs. It's the height. Brown hair, blue eyes, and 34 years old as stated. I am a nonsmoker and very light social drinker and I seek the same. I enjoy animals and I am currently owned by a cat. I enjoy a good non-horror movie and dining out, but they are a lot more fun if done with someone. I enjoy building clocks and have been known to chase a train or two. If after reading this you think I have made it inside your parameters, you can give me a call. Usually home by 9:00 p.m. Home sooner most days but to be safe, I am home by then most nights. We can talk and see what happens from there. Thank you very much for your time. Thanks. Gordon

I lay the letters aside for the moment. I need to think and pray about this before I actually make up my mind to contact any of them. I decide to take the letters along to work and let some of my coworkers read them. I hope they will give me their input. I have no problem getting them interested in my potential love life. The consensus is that I should contact Gordon.

Friday, on my day off, I turn the issue over and over in my mind. *Should I call him, or shouldn't I?* Finally, with shaking hands, I take a deep breath and dial the number.

"Hello?" he answers almost immediately. His voice is strong, confident, and pleasant.

We chat for a while, and I roll around in my mind if I should tell him that I am Mennonite. I don't really want him to be shocked out of his mind when he sees me. We agree to meet at Perkins Restaurant in Superior, a neutral place, the following Sunday.

"And you'll recognize me by the little white cap I wear and my dress. I'm Mennonite."

He hesitates a moment and then says, "I don't really know much about Mennonites, but I'll see you then."

He tells me later that if it hadn't been for the promise that he had made to himself when he began placing personal ads and now in answering them to take out any lady who responded to his contacts, he would not have shown up. To himself, he said, "This is going to be one fast lunch."

So what is the problem that looms so large? I am Mennonite and he is Lutheran. And so begins our religious journey together – a journey that takes us into a different denomination altogether and into the seemingly seamless mingling of two separate pasts.

∞∞∞∞

Mennonites are distinguishable from other Protestant denominations primarily by several practices that are distinct. They were, historically, called Anabaptists because of their rejection of infant baptism and the exercise of re-baptism of consenting adult believers. The Mennonite Christian is to be separate from the world in all areas of life. This translates into a strict belief in the separation of church and state, and the practice of non-resistance. This position in 1524 of the Anabaptists, under the leadership of Menno Simons, was in direct opposition to the position of other reformers. Other reformers such as Martin Luther, John Calvin, Ulrich Zwingli, and John Knox followed the position of the Catholic Church which was that the government had the right to legislate the spiritual belief system of the people.[1](Global Anabaptist Mennonite Encyclopedia Online)

No conservative Mennonite church member may serve in the military, participate in a lawsuit, vote, or hold public office. Dressing differently from the world is also stressed. For women, this means they are not to "use makeup, cut their hair, and wear slacks, shorts, or fashionable head dress, short sleeves, low necklines, dresses not reaching well below the knees, or clothes that expose the form of the body in an immodest way. The hair is to be covered with a veil of sufficient size to adequately cover the head."[2] (Excerpted from the Statement of Christian Doctrine and Rules and Discipline, Lancaster Conference of the Mennonite Church, July 17, 1968.)

Basic beliefs, though, are similar to most mainline Protestant churches. Mennonites believe that salvation is by grace alone through faith alone on the basis of Scripture alone and that scripture is the final authority on all matters of faith. They believe in the Trinity, that Jesus is the Son of God, and that He died on the cross to save us from our sins.

Just as the Mennonite does, the Protestant Missouri Synod Lutheran holds to the same doctrine of justification by grace alone through faith alone on the basis of Scripture alone. He believes the doctrine that scripture is the final authority on all matters of faith. He believes in the Trinity, that Jesus is the Son of God, and that Jesus died on the cross to save us from our sins.

The Missouri Synod Lutheran church is a small, socially conservative branch of Lutheranism which has maintained separation from the larger ELCA or Evangelical Lutheran Church in America. Fundamental identifiers are that they claim a literalist interpretation of the Bible and practice closed or "close" Communion, believing that total doctrinal agreement is necessary amongst communicants. They do not accept women into the ordained priesthood and are extremely conservative on doctrinal and social issues. All of these beliefs, I find to be similar to those held by those in my own Mennonite background. There is nothing that Gordon and I disagree on with the EXCEPTION of one - baptism. The Lutheran church practices the baptism of infants.[3]

Still, pre-conceived prejudices and cultural stigmas lurk in our brains. I believe that converting to Lutheranism would be a step in the wrong direction. It has always been impressed upon me that only Mennonites are following the true interpretations of scripture. And not surprisingly, Gordon has been taught the same thing in his Lutheran tradition.

∞∞∞∞

Our "fast" lunch at Perkins on May 6, 1990 turns into a long afternoon walk at a local park. "Why do you trust me that you will go walking in the woods alone with me on our first date?" is Gordon's question.

"I don't know." I respond. I am enthralled with this man I have met and feelings that I have never had swirl around inside of me. When we finally part, I go home with a desire to meet this man again. I am torn by what I know this could mean. Gordon has told me that he has no desire to ever become Mennonite, but I can't seem to stop myself in this thrill that has sucked me into its grip.

As the months of 1990 roll by and we continue dating, this question of how to assimilate our faith beliefs under one common denomination remains an issue. On July 29, just three months into our relationship, Gordon invites me to visit his Lutheran church in Algona, MN. We arrive a few minutes before the service and slip into a back pew.

Everyone reverently sits quietly waiting for the service to start while organ music plays in the background. It is a beautiful church with different scenes from the life of Christ incorporated into the stain glass windows. The altar boys soon softly tread down the aisle to light the candles on the altar. I glance at the bulletin we have been given. Every part of the service and the wording for each has been detailed in it. Soon, we begin what for me feels like a series of "sit down-standup" activities of singing, reciting, and responding. *I guess I won't go to sleep in this church.* The structure of worship seems rigid compared to what I am used to. I am beginning to learn that this is what is called a highly liturgical structure of worship. The question I must answer is, "Can I find this meaningful if I pursue this relationship with Gordon and he is not willing to change churches?" Love does crazy things to people so part of me wants to convince myself that I can make this adjustment if truly necessary but another part of me wants to search for a more middle-of-the-road compromise for both of us.

I begin to research beliefs and to visit different churches in Superior, MN. I am not sure what eventually draws me to the Evangelical Free Church there, but I am impressed. The people are friendly, there is lots of visiting and chatter before the service and the service flows with a freedom that I find comforting. The service style is quite similar to the Mennonite services that I am familiar with. I, personally, start attending this church while Gordon continues to attend the Lutheran church in Algoma where he is highly connected, counting the offering after each service and being part of the church council.

We have many discussions about our faith backgrounds and if this is an area in which we are incompatible. "We are not going to attend separate churches if we get married," I impress on him. In this, I am resolute. He is concerned about the reaction of his parents and insists that our children must be baptized. *OK, what's a little water on the head of a child,* I reason, *it won't help them, but it won't hurt them either if this is what it takes for a compromise.* I finally convince Gordon to accompany me to the EFC in Superior on February 3 of 1991. He asks me to marry him the following week on February 14. We begin to attend membership classes at the EFC shortly thereafter and to commence our marriage counseling there as well. But we still alternate between the Lutheran church in Algoma and the Free Church in Superior for Sunday services.

"What are you going to do if Gordon refuses to change churches," the pastor inquires of me.

"I will become Lutheran," I respond. It is not what I want (and I haven't told Gordon this) but I am prepared to do so because I love this man. During the process of our marriage counseling, the pastor informs us that there is a fairly new Evangelical Free Church in Corinth which is about five miles from where we will be living.

"You should check it out and maybe even plan to have your wedding there." He says.

On May 19, 1991, Gordon and I visit the Evangelical Free Church in Corinth, Mn for the first time. The people are friendly and welcoming. The problem, as far as a wedding there, is that the kitchen is not finished. It is not even a year since this church broke ground on their building. This is a new congregation having just been accepted into the Evangelical Free Church of America the month before. It is an exciting time for this church. If we even knew this information at the time, we did not give the fact of them being a new church plant much of a second thought. We are wrapped up in our own exciting times and are pretty oblivious to the enthusiasm of this baby congregation. I do know that I cannot get married in an unfinished church. We continue with our wedding plans at the EFC in Superior but do take to heart the encouragement to make the EFC in Corinth our spiritual home. We read through the Statement of Beliefs that seems generic to most evangelistic Christian denominations. There are no legalistic rules or regulations that need to be followed. We are happy with the freedom this church grants us in our faith.

ARTICLE III: Doctrinal Statements of Faith
Truth Evangelical Free Church

WE BELIEVE:

1. The Scriptures, both Old and New Testaments, to be the inspired Word of God, without error in the original writings, the complete revelation of His will for the salvation of men and the Divine and final authority for Christian faith and life. [2 Timothy 3:16; 1 Peter 1:25]

2. In one God, Creator of all things, infinitely perfect and eternally existing in three persons: Father, Son, and Holy Spirit.
[Deuteronomy 6:4; Isaiah 45:5; John 1:1; Acts 5: 3-4]

3. That Jesus Christ is true God and true man, having been conceived of the Holy Spirit and born of the Virgin Mary. He died on the cross a sacrifice for our sins according to the Scriptures. Further, He arose bodily from the dead, ascended into heaven, where at the right hand of the Majesty on High, He is now our High Priest and Advocate.
[Matthew 1: 18-23; Luke 24: 50-53; John 1:14; 1 Corinthians 15: 3-4; 1 John 2:1]

4. That the ministry of the Holy Spirit is to glorify the Lord Jesus Christ, and during this age to convict men, regenerate the believing sinner, indwell, guide, instruct and empower the believer for godly living and service.
[John 16: 8-11; 11-26]

5. That man was created in the image of God but fell into sin and is therefore lost and only through regeneration by the Holy Spirit can salvation and spiritual life be obtained.
[Genesis 1:27; Romans 5: 12-21, Titus 3: 5-6]

6. That the shed blood of Jesus Christ and His resurrection provide the only ground for justification and salvation for all who believe, and only such as receive Jesus Christ are born of the Holy Spirit and, thus, become children of God.
[2 Corinthians 5:21; Hebrews 9: 11-14]

7. That water baptism and the Lord's Supper are ordinances to be observed by the Church during the present age. They are, however, not to be regarded as means of salvation.
[Romans 6: 1-10; 1 Corinthians 11: 23-26]

8. That the true Church is composed of all such persons who through saving faith in Jesus Christ have been regenerated by the Holy Spirit and are united together in the body of Christ of which He is the Head.
[1 Corinthians 12:13; Galatians 3: 26-29; Ephesians 1:22]

9. That only those who are thus members of the true Church shall be eligible for membership in the local church.
[1 Corinthians 1: 1-4; 1 Peter 1: 1-3]

10. That Jesus Christ is the Lord and Head of the Church, and that every local church has the right under Christ to decide and govern its own affairs.
[1 Peter 2: 4-5; Matthew 18: 15-18]

11. In the personal premillennial and imminent coming of our Lord Jesus Christ and that this "Blessed Hope" has a vital bearing on the personal life and service of the believer.

[Revelation 20: 1-3; Titus 2: 13]

12. In the bodily resurrection of the dead; of the believer to everlasting blessedness and joy with the Lord, of the unbeliever to judgment and everlasting conscious punishment.

[1 Corinthians 15: 50-57; 1 John 3:2; Revelation 20: 11-13]

Chapter 2 Settling Into Life In Our New Church

Gordon walks up the steps to the baptismal tank installed at the front of the church with a towel draped over his arm. He is dressed in jeans and a light cotton shirt. He descends into the tank where Pastor Wayne waits for him along with an elder of the church.

"I baptize you in the name of the Father, the Son, and the Holy Spirit."

The words resound across the congregation just before Gordon is lowered beneath the water. Gordon has chosen to be re-baptized into his Christian faith as an adult after a couple of years under the teaching of Pastor Wayne.

We have both been able to make the transition from our former faith traditions into the Evangelical Free Church tradition. At first, our involvement in the church is simply an attending of the Sunday morning services. Gordon gets up and leaves as soon as the words of the last song have died away. He struggles with building new relationships. He struggles with the loss of the roles that he held in his former church. I feel guilty for taking him away from his established faith practice and wonder if he will ever be able to make the change. But core people continue to reach out to us. We find out that Pastor Wayne has a background in electrical contracting and this builds a bridge between him and Gordon. Finally, as time goes by, we start to feel more comfortable. We do not participate in most of the extracurricular activities, but we eventually begin to feel accepted. Today's baptism marks a major transition in Gordon's comfort level and acceptance in the church. It also erases any concern that I have had about what to do about baptizing our children. Our tiny daughter, born in 1993, will be allowed to make her own decision to be baptized into the faith when she is old enough to understand the claims of Christ.

Around this time also, we join Truth Evangelical Free Church. It is an informal affair of being welcomed as members by Pastor Wayne with a box of ice cream in front of the congregation. We are officially ushered in with a public unanimous "Yea" vote of the members. We do not sign any kind of membership agreement nor are we required to give our testimony in front of the congregation. This is how I picture a church to be – a loosely knit group of Christians who support each other, challenge each other, worship together, play together, and make decisions as equals following the principles of the Bible. We agree with the church's purpose statement "As enabled by the Holy Spirit, TEFC seeks to glorify the Father through spiritual growth of believers so that others may be led to a saving faith in Jesus Christ as directed by God through the Bible. Therefore, we practice and encourage the following: Prayer, Study of God's Word, Sharing the Gospel, Fellowship with believers and Worship."

In 1994, Gordon and I volunteer to teach Sunday School class together for the 6th – 8th grade early adolescents. Gordon works hard each week to develop a lesson that includes a craft, a spiritual lesson, or the learning of the basic tenants of Christianity (The Lord's Prayer, The Ten Commandments, etc) which many of the young people seem to lack. At the end of the year, we sponsor a picnic and hike to the County Park. There the kids compete for the privilege of carrying and entertaining our 2-year-old daughter, Erin. We enjoy the spirited enthusiasm of the young ones and continue to teach this age group throughout the next two years.

The end of 1994 brings the question to Gordon, "Will you put your name on the ballot for elder?" At this point in time, there is only one governing board composed of four elders and four deacons; all men. Gordon is not sure that he is ready to take on this role but after much prayer and soul searching, he agrees to have his name placed on the ballot. At the annual meeting at the end of January 1995, he is elected. Within four years' time, we have assimilated into a new church and moved into the inner circle. We did not think of it, at that time, as any special position. We see ourselves as well as all the other members of the church as "sinners saved by grace" struggling along in the kingdom together.

As with any church, conditions are not always as happy under the surface as they appear to be from the outside. Often one doesn't see these imperfections and relationship blips until becoming immersed in the system. One of the members who is on the elder board and who also holds the position of treasurer is accused of moving cattle out of his feedlot where he is feeding them and selling them without the knowledge of the owner. He is charged with theft and spends a few days in jail. As in all small churches and communities, there is much conflicting information as to what the actual truth is. Rumors and accusations swirl around the community and the church. Eventually this situation leads this gentleman to resign his eldership and treasurer role in June 1995. The ultimate result of this situation is that the reputation of the church in the community has been tarnished, making it difficult to attract new families.

As we move into 1996, Pastor Wayne makes a rather unexpected resignation announcement from the pastorate. Prior to this, his daughter had discovered that she had breast cancer while pregnant. She refused treatment but was able to give birth to a healthy child. However, she dies a few months later, leaving her children motherless and husband without a companion. Pastor Wayne and his wife feel called to move closer to them to help out. The church is suddenly without a pastor. Gordon, as an elder, is asked to serve on the search committee for a new pastor. And so, begins a very busy year with many evenings taken up by elder meetings and search committee meetings. As the wife of an elder, I also throw myself into the task of typing surveys for the congregation, analyzing data, and preparing letters as needed. All of the hard work of the search committee results in the coming of a new pastor, Pastor Frank, in October.

During this year of participating in the search for a new pastor, Gordon and I continue to teach the 6th – 8th grade Sunday School class. Towards the end of this year, I am contacted by one of the deaconesses.

"Would you consider being a deaconess?"

I hesitate. I am not a social person and I have no idea what this role requires. The Deaconess Handbook describes deaconesses as "women chosen from among the church membership, who are regular attenders, serving the Lord through the care of the church body. They support the church and demonstrate spiritual growth with their lives confirming 1 Timothy 3: 11 'in the same way, their wives are to be women worthy of respect, not malicious talkers but temperate and trustworthy in everything.'"

"What does a deaconess do? I question.

"There are three deaconesses. Each year a new deaconess comes on the board. The first year, we will try to limit your duties and just sort of train the new person. Each year, you take on a little more responsibility. These are the things the deaconesses take care of:

*Any concerns of the church body – helping those in need. This is a very general job that we are just to be aware of

*Setting up Spring/Fall Cleaning of the Church

*Getting communion ready

*Providing meals/showers for those who need the service (We only make sure it is done by someone)

*Social Events such as potlucks – make sure people are there to help clean-up/set-up

*Women's Ministry leader – We approve the activities she leads and take things to the board if we think it needs to be discussed by them.

*This year we will also be generating ideas on how to incorporate the theme this year. It is 'The family.' Pastor wants us to come up with some ideas for the church to possibly do."

Wow, that sounds overwhelming, but I agree with much reservation, to try this new role. Gordon and I love this church and are more than happy to serve the Lord and work for its furtherment. Gordon has grown in his faith tremendously while being on the elder board. We both feel accepted and a part of this little church community.

Chapter 3 In the Inner Circle

Throughout this time of church interaction in 1996, we have also, in our personal lives, been constructing a new house on forty acres of land. In February of 1997, a group of men show up from Truth to move our belongings into our new home.

As both of us are now members of the leadership team at church, we are caught up, as well, in an undercurrent of turmoil that swirls about the church. The gentleman who resigned from the elder board in 1995 after charges of theft has now moved into financial management during which he recruits fellow church members and others in the community to buy overseas stocks with the promise that their investments will generate a high percentage of return. He collects thousands of dollars and soon after builds a castle in the country. Rumors circulate that he has taken everyone's money to build his house. Gordon has a unique connection to this upheaval as he provides the electrical wiring for the house. All charges are denied by the man. The anger in the community and in the church builds even further when people realize that their investment is not yielding returns, or the principal being returned to them when desired. Some families leave the church and the church now has a huge shadow over it. Once people find out that this gentleman is a part of our church, they want nothing to do with it. The image in the community is one of mistrust and skepticism. The leadership struggles to decide what is the Biblical response to this situation that they cannot rightly judge from afar. Do they ex-communicate this member from the church? No one has ever ex-communicated someone from this church? That seems rather drastic. Or do they treat him like a sinner – ie try to love him back as you would a non-Christian. There is division, as well, amongst the elder/deacon board in the church and no definitive action is ever taken.

∞∞∞

So what theologically in concise terms is it that we believe in this little church? First, man is totally depraved, spiritually dead in his sins, and blind, but that doesn't mean he is unable to repent or call out to be saved. Man is a sinner who has the free will to either accept God's call to salvation or not. God wants everyone to be saved but will only save those who call out to Him of their own free will. When Christ died on the cross, He shed His blood for everyone but only those who believe in Him will receive His salvation. Saving grace can be resisted because God won't overrule man's free will. Man is born again when he believes and receives God's grace. At least this is what I have always believed, and these seem to be the prominent beliefs of others in this church. Neither Gordon nor I are aware that a new movement is blooming in our backyard that will rock our world in a few years.

A man named John Piper became pastor of Bethlehem Baptist Church in Minneapolis in 1980 after teaching at Bethel University and Seminary in St Paul, MN for six years. He exploded as an influence on the evangelical scene after the publication of his book, *Desiring God: Meditations of a Christian Hedonist,* in 1986.[4]

According to Roger Olson, on his blog Patheos,

I first became aware of the Young, Restless, Reformed Movement (YRRM) before anyone thought to give it that moniker. I was teaching theology at Baptist-related Bethel College and Seminary (now Bethel University) in Minnesota. John Piper had left the faculty to take the pulpit at nearby Bethlehem Baptist Church about a year before I arrived. He was still much discussed by students and faculty alike and seemed to have been a polarizing figure on campus. People tended either to love him or despise him. I had read his article about "Christian Hedonism" in HIS magazine (the now defunct publication of the InterVarsity Christian Fellowship) before then and had met Piper when I first visited Bethel a few years before joining its faculty...

Not long after taking my teaching position at Bethel I began to hear colleagues calling certain students (mostly males) "Piper Cubs." It wasn't long before I could identify them myself. They tended to quote Piper a lot and be passionate about Calvinism. One told me I wasn't a Christian because I wasn't a Calvinist!

Over the following years (approximately 1984 to 1999) I witnessed the beginnings of the YRRM. It was born and then grew and coalesced around Piper's pastoral conferences at Bethlehem Baptist Church.[5]

Piper wrote many books but one of the ones that would become especially influential was co-edited with Wayne Grudem called *Recovering Biblical Manhood and Womanhood*. It was published in 1991 for the Council on Biblical Manhood.[4]

But, of course, we know nothing about any of these events that will come to affect our lives over the next dozen years. At Truth, there is not really an official position on the place of women in the church. Women lead Bible

Studies, prayer groups, teach adult and children's Sunday School and are treated as equals with the exception of being prohibited from being on the leadership board. There is a friendly discussion, though, and a call for women to be allowed to participate more in the life of the church. Women want to have more input into the decisions of the church. A discussion at the church picnic soon after Pastor Frank's arrival in 1996 focused on the role of women in the church. This leads to discussions regarding women serving on the Board and the topic being included on the Board agenda. A committee is formed to study the scriptures and to research what other churches are doing. From this comes a position paper on the Role of Women in the Church and the recommendation to restructure the leadership into two Boards. The Board's desire is to broaden the base of leadership in the church. It is the opinion of the men on the Elder board that the church will be healthier with many people sharing the work load of the church. Having two boards will "allow the women a more significant role in the operation of the church, encourage a broader range of involvement of our members and allow for more time (for the elders) to deal with the spiritual life of the church."

Thus, at the annual meeting on January 3, 1999, a new structure for the church is approved by the congregation and the Constitution is changed soon after. Gordon, in the last,
year of his elder term, and I, as a deaconess, have had an instrumental role in making this change. I, as a woman feel needed and wanted here while still following the Biblical mandate for the men to lead. There will now be an Elder board consisting of four men whose job it is to care for the spiritual needs of the congregation and "oversee all the activities of the church" and an Administrative Council

made up of seven people who will have the responsibility of "overseeing ministry implementation and all property and fiscal matters." There must be at least two men and two women. The remaining three members can be either male or female.[6] An underlying principle inserted in the constitution from the beginning is left intact – "The Pastor shall be a **non-voting** member of both the Elder Board and the Administrative Council." This is to protect the church from a pastor who might want to be authoritarian.

Under the new structure, Gordon is also re-elected to the elder role for a three-year term. As the deaconess role has been eliminated, I step into the dual roles of Children's Sunday School Superintendent and Children's Church Coordinator. Our daughter is now five years old making these roles especially pertinent to me and what teaching I want to see the children experience. I choose and purchase the curriculum, secure the teachers needed, and make sure each Sunday is staffed. Erin also attends the very active AWANA program that is held on Wednesday evenings. On top of this, we host a small group Bible Study at our home on Sunday evenings. We have integrated well into the Evangelical Free Church. We are part of the inner circle.

It is during 1999 that Gordon begins a role that he will become sought after and well known for in this church for fifteen years. Vacation Bible School is coming up and the committee is looking for someone to coordinate decorating. The curriculum is using a space theme for teaching. Gordon spends hours in his shop converting electrical panels, heating pipe, electrical wire, and miscellaneous junk into Mama, Papa, and Baby space aliens.

But all is not rosy at church. There remains the

Summary

Role of Women in the Church

Consideration of the role of women in the church in today's climate is tension-filled and potentially dangerous. A discussion of this volatile subject could be divisive and thwart the effectiveness of the church. On the other hand, a full and thorough discussion in a loving manner, attended with prayer, could open up a whole new understanding and dynamic of ministry. We must not only respect one another and the differing opinions we bring to the table, we must genuinely love and uphold one another. This could be liberating and constructive. If, for example, some women are under false constraints, a biblical clarification can bring release and freedom. Likewise, if men have become domineering and callous to the needs of their wives, and women in general, corrective steps can lead to healing and true biblical leadership.

There is equality of male and female. God established equality at the very beginning when He created male & female, Gen 1:26-28: *Then God said, "Let us make man in our image, in our likeness, and let them rule over the fish of the sea and the birds of the air, over the livestock, over all the earth, and over all the creatures that move along the ground." So God created man in his own image, in the image of God he created him; male and female he created them. God blessed them and said to them, "Be fruitful and increase in number; fill the earth and subdue it. Rule over the fish of the sea and the birds of the air and over every living creature that moves on the ground."* He personally created Adam and Eve in His own image. He gave them a high calling to rule over the created order. This equality extends to their spiritual nature. Both sinned and were judged. Men and women, alike, have been offered the same salvation in Christ.

Male headship in marriage is also a foundational teaching of the Bible. His headship is rooted in the created order and a direct mandate of God. There is no inconsistency or incompatibility of male-female equality and male headship. Headship does not suggest superiority of a man or inferiority of a woman. Male headship does follow a pattern ordained in the Bible. Headship and submission is even true of the functional economy of the godhead, 1 Cor 11:3, *Now I want you to realize that the head of every man is Christ, and the head of the woman is man, and the head of Christ is God.*

God has called men and women to vital service for Him. There are a variety of ministries both men and women fulfill. Service, and the kind of service, requires meeting God's requirements. There is no intimation given that a man has a head start or an edge over a woman. The Bible considers and shares how both men and women have been uniquely and fruitfully used of the Lord. We know from experience that women often make up the majority of churches. Women consistently are the most spiritually awake in the church. There are two offices in the church where women are restricted, the pastor and elder. 1 Timothy 3:1-7 and Titus 1:5-9 calls for men to fulfill the office of elder. 1 Timothy 3:1-7: *Here is a trustworthy saying: If anyone sets his heart on being an overseer, he desires a noble task. Now the overseer must be above reproach, the husband of but one wife, temperate, self-controlled, respectable, hospitable, able to teach, not given to drunkenness, not violent but gentle, not quarrelsome, not a lover of money. He must manage his own family well and see that his children obey him with proper respect. (If anyone does not know how to manage his own family, how can he take care of God's church?) He must not be a recent convert, or he may become conceited and fall under the same judgment as the devil. He must also have a good reputation with outsiders, so that he will not fall into disgrace and into the devil's trap.* Titus 1:5-9: *The reason I left you in Crete was that you might straighten out what was left unfinished and appoint elders in every town, as I directed you. An elder must be blameless, the husband of but one wife, a man whose children believe and are not open to the charge of being wild and disobedient. Since an overseer is entrusted with God's work, he must be blameless-- not overbearing, not quick-tempered, not given to drunkenness, not violent, not pursuing dishonest gain. Rather he must be hospitable, one who loves what is good, who is self-controlled, upright, holy and disciplined. He must hold firmly to the trustworthy message as it has been taught, so that he can encourage others by sound doctrine and refute those who oppose it.* Scripture also restricts women from pastor, specifically preaching, 1 Tim 2:11-15. *A woman should learn in quietness and full submission. I do not permit a woman to teach or to have authority over a man; she must be silent. For Adam was formed first, then Eve. And Adam was not the one deceived; it was the woman who was deceived and became a sinner. But women will be saved through childbearing--if they continue in faith, love and holiness with propriety.* We follow many conservative Bible teachers by understanding this passage to take "teaching" to mean preaching and the authorative proclamation of the Word. It does not refer to teaching a Bible Study or Sunday School class. 1 Corinthians 14:33b-36 (limits the authority of women

underlying problem with the man whose investments are not returning any profit, let alone the outrageously promised high profits. This leads to continued hard feelings between members in the church and in the community towards the church. Pastor Frank is becoming discouraged and disheartened. He presents his vision of building a healthy church, but he often finds himself sitting alone at prayer meetings. Pastor Frank expresses his feelings at the annual meeting.

We began the year 2000 with great expectations. Potential appeared high. I should have understood God's perspective from James 4:13, 14a better. Look here, you people who say, "Today or tomorrow we are going to a certain town and will stay a year. We will do business there and make a profit." How do you know what will happen tomorrow? It is humbling to know that even when things look good we do not know whether it will continue. We have no way of knowing what lies beyond the next bend in the road. But what appears to be bleak, even painful, is fully directed by our loving Lord.

We did fall short of anticipated growth. There were several reasons for this: (1) We lost five families totaling nineteen people during the first half of the year; many in significant leadership posts, (2) potentially significant spiritual initiatives were not realized (community survey, prayer opportunities, missions), (3) others left our fellowship, some permanently... There is an undercurrent of negativity. Is it a spirit of discontent, bitterness or discouragement? Maybe people are weary of the work. Regardless, it is discouraging to find those willing to do the work of ministry while many are content to sit on the sidelines.[7]

In the middle of this year, Gordon finds himself catapulted into the Chairman position on the Elder Board. In his own words.

I assumed the responsibilities of Chairman of the Elder Board in June due to the current chairman resigning to take a new job in Iowa. I had, at one time, thought being chairman of the board would be a position to aspire to. But then I took a serious look at the requirements of the job and came to the conclusion that there was no way I was qualified, and I did not want the job. In fact, I was kind of relieved that the former chairman was chosen in January to head up the board. Then he was gone and being Vice-chairman, the job became mine by default. I now feel even less qualified to lead God's people.

This is our second full year of having two boards and I believe the change has given the Elders more time to be concerned with the spiritual health of the church. We always seem to have enough to do. More open communication with the Administrative Council is still something we need to work on so that together we are going in the same direction.

Last year, the former chairman urged us to pray as a church and personally. I hope you have taken his urging to heart this past year and continue to pray into the new year. The leaders of the church need your prayers and support. My daughter, Erin, at seven years old prays every night that she would "be good," that her mom and dad would "be good," and that her grandma would "be good," and that her friends would "be good." I don't believe that she is praying that God would make their behavior good but that she is praying for the health and welfare of everyone that is important to her. Taking Isaiah 11:6 "...and a little child shall lead them" to heart, I pray that you (all the church body) "be good" both health wise and spiritually in the new year."[7]

Another position is also abruptly vacated in the middle of the year 2000 – that of treasurer of the church, a spot on the newly formed Administrative Council. Though I am still acting as the Children's Sunday School Superintendent, I am asked to fill this position. No one else wants to be treasurer. Managing finances has always been one of my strengths and I have always said that my second choice of employment would have been accounting. I receive no orientation as this was a hastily vacated position, so I pick up the books and convert everything over to Quicken as one of my first projects. I love this job. I feel needed and others on the Administrative Council listen to my advice and recommendations.

∞∞∞

A fire leaps in streaks of orange into the sky. A few slaps at mosquitos resound occasionally. Laughter and chatter fill the evening air as we are joined around the campfire by two families from church. This is what many weekends in our summer consist of. As chairman of the board and treasurer respectively, Gordon and I have many responsibilities at church. Gordon began to sense the restlessness and discontent of Pastor Frank. "He is going to be leaving soon," is his prediction at the beginning of 2001. Sure enough in June, Pastor Frank resigns abruptly and moves away. The small congregation of around fifty members struggles spiritually and emotionally. The church has a negative reputation in the community. Everyone is discouraged. There is talk of closing the church. Gordon, consequently, with the help of the Holy Spirit rises to the task of guiding the church. "We are not going to let the devil win. We are going to come together to pray again and seek the face of the Lord," he declares. He begins a plan for the elders to meet with each family in the church over the next couple of months to get a feel for how people think things are going. Gordon hopes to offer an opportunity for members to give expression to the simmering discontent that has never been resolved as a result of the gentleman who has collected investment monies and never provided any returns. Open discussion also provides a good starting point for the newly formed search committee as they develop a profile of the church.

With his creative talent, Gordon provides and supervises the decorating again for summer Vacation Bible School. The theme is a western one. A horse made out of cardboard greets the children as they arrive. The sanctuary is transformed into a town with a general store, a community center, and rows of straw bales for sitting upon while learning lessons about the gospel.

Chapter 4 Gordon's Testimony As He Leads the Church

The year of 2002 finds the search committee working diligently to find and review potential candidates for the position of senior pastor. Gordon spends many hours at church in the evenings as Chairman of the Search Committee and Chairman of the Elder Board. Some people begin to think he is the pastor. He also fills the pulpit for the first time ever.

Good Morning!

Look around you. The people you see with totally shocked looks on their faces know me too well. The worried looking ones know me. Those with the "I wonder what's going on look" have seen me around before and the normal looking ones don't know me at all or as the others would say, "they are the truly blessed."

For the shocked, I am shocked also. It is out of character for me to be up here at least at this time of the service. For the worried, you can stop worrying too much because I ran my talk past Pastor Les to make sure my theology wasn't totally off base. And for the other two groups, by the end of my speech you will, for better or for worse, know some more about my family and me. I have taught children's Sunday School, facilitated adult Sunday School, helped with nursery and children's church, been an elder, helped with communion, sound, and announcements but I have never tried to say anything meaningful in front of a group of people before. I feel a lot like the baseball player who has played most of the positions except pitching and today that player gets to pitch for the first time.

For those of you who don't know, my name is Gordon Farmer. My family and I have attended this church for ten years now. We have great friendships in this group and it is a joy for us to worship and serve God with you here. As I may never be allowed to do this again, not to mention that I may never have the courage to get back up here, I intend to take full advantage of this time here this morning.

I have an antidotal way of looking at life that I would like to try to explain to you after which I would like to tell you my testimony of how God has worked in my life - perhaps even how I got up here. Along the way, I may mix in a couple suggestions and at the end, I will leave just a little something for you to think about.

I agree with Kent Hovind when he says, "I believe the Bible cover to cover. It is the inerrant word of God." Dr. Hovind is a creation scientist who speaks all over the world on creation, science, and dinosaurs. The adult Sunday School class, as well as one of the small groups, is currently watching his tapes. The youth have watched them in the last year also. They are a refreshing change from all the evolution preached at us in the secular media. I would be glad to share the tapes with anyone here, as I believe that if we cannot accept creation as truth then we cannot accept Jesus dying on the cross for us as truth.

One of the most astonishing things to me when we started coming to this church was that the people actually brought their Bibles to church with them. All the churches I had previously attended printed the verses for the service on the back of the bulletin and the bulletin came from the home denomination. No one brought a Bible to church. I suppose this was done so that all were taught the same and it seemed reasonable at the time. I now would feel empty with no Bible on the way to church. I would ask you to please continue to bring your Bible to worship with you. Since I am not a preacher (which will soon become very evident), I will not be talking today using any one Bible verse or text, so you probably will not have a lot of use for your Bible today. But I thank you for bringing them.

Some of you know of my fondness for trains. Tie that fondness together with my love of God and you come up with the following analogy. In the days of steam trains, there was a little car at the end of all trains called the caboose and in that caboose was the conductor. He told the engineer when to start up, when to stop, how fast to go etc. He did the paper work and in effect, ran the train. The engineer did what the conductor told him to do when he told him to do it. This prevented accidents and allowed the train to make all the right stops. Now if you will consider with me that life is like a train. You are the engineer and Jesus is the conductor back there in the caboose. Now consider a Christian family; the husband drives the first engine, the wife the second, and the children come next. They are all coupled onto the cars behind them which are full of freight. The freight is the little and big sins we pull around like jealousy, envy, self-centeredness, unkindness, the list goes on. The more cars behind the engines, the harder the pull is for the family and the further from Jesus in the caboose they can become. Anyone in the family can add a car to the train; the children by disobedience, rebellion, etc or the parents by bad decisions in life.

Some young people start out in life with lots of freight. They leave home at about twenty years of age and uncouple their engine from their family but take along all the freight cars of jealousy, drugs, drinking, immoral behavior, etc that they have collected while they were "having fun." It could be a long train and hard to pull alone. Sometimes, they forget to take a caboose with them and therefore do not have Jesus directing their train. The results can be disastrous.

If you have a caboose with Jesus, the conductor, in it and you are listening to Him then Jesus will tell you how and on which sidings you can dump off some of your heavy freight cars. Pulling your train will grow easier as your train grows shorter and your load lighter. You will be growing closer to Jesus. But if you do not listen to Jesus, then your train will grow long and hard to pull. It will be hard to hear Jesus in the distance. Yet Jesus is still back there in the caboose and wanting to help you get rid of your freight cars and help you grow closer to him. If you let him, he can help you lighten your load and of course, Jesus and that caboose are there whether or not you want Him to be, if you have accepted Him in your heart. When you are ready to listen to Him, he is there and willing to help. In Hebrews 13:5, it says, "I will never leave you nor forsake you."

When you get ready to marry, the Christian or anyone for that matter, should look at the train that your prospective mate is pulling. That's basically what you are doing with dating. Does he or she have carloads of drugs or sexual partners, drinking, rage, immorality, etc.? Do you want to couple your train to theirs and help pull all that stuff along? The Bible says in II Corinthians 6:14, "Be not unequally yoked." Can you image what kind of wreck you could get into if you hooked two steam engines together and they didn't pull the same direction? At the least, you would get no place. At the worst, things would blow up. So once you have gotten married, the woman in a Christian marriage couples her engine in behind his and they become one train. They both pull together listening to Jesus, neither more important than the other, and the train pulls easier than it did when each pulled their own. Then along comes a baby. At first, the child just rides. As he or she grows, he begins to add his own cars to the train - not many if he becomes a Christian and honors his father and mother. If not and he gets into immorality, drugs, and other sins, then the train has many more cars and the load is heavier for his parents and him. The train may even pull apart in places. Many times, it seems to this family like Jesus in the caboose is far away.

As the Christian couple grows older, the family leaves to start their own trains and Jesus can seem closer. Even when you are way off track, if you listen to Jesus in the caboose, He as the good conductor can get you back on the right track. It is never too late to listen to the Good Conductor. Even if you wreck the train, He can get you back on track. A Christian life is spent trying to get closer to Jesus in the caboose. We can never remove all the cars between Him and us, but we can dump some on the sidings along the way. By only listening to Jesus can you get on the right track to Heaven. In John 14:6 Jesus said, "I am the Way, the Truth, and the Life. No man comes unto the Father except through me." Only Jesus is the Way. As for me when the time comes, I want that caboose as close as possible, so I can listen to the conductor as He intercedes for me with the great train conductor in heaven and because of Jesus, the controller will throw the right switch to get me into the great rail yard of heaven.

Some of you may be saying to yourself, "This is too simple." and that is possible. But I believe the analogy about the train is worth considering. I can tell you that sometimes in my life, my caboose has been almost out of sight back there. It has grown closer since I have been coming here. There are a lot of engineers in this church who have very few cars between them and the caboose that have been great examples for me and I thank God for them.

I grew up in a mainline denominational church. I haven't gone far from home. Until recently, I thought everyone was a Christian. All my aunts and uncles went to the same church my parents and I attended. There were about fifteen cousins, counting my siblings, and I as well as all those I hung out with at school that went to church - most to the one I attended. In 1969,

I went through a confirmation course and all my life until sometime in my early 30's, I thought I was a Christian. My late twenty's and early thirties were a very bad time emotionally and spiritually. Deep utter loneliness set in. I started to spend some time in the bar and drink as my boss spent most of his time there. One night after drinking too much, I drove home from Algoma to Bartlett – about twenty-five miles. I got up in the morning and could not remember driving home yet there was my car outside. It really scared me. I moved to Algoma, so I wouldn't have to drive but I knew I didn't want to be like that and I wasn't yet a heavy drinker, so I determined to stop spending time at the bar. My boss continued to spend many hours there. He would call me at night with a service call and I would have to finish the sentence for him, so he could get it across to me where I needed to go. Because of his influence, more than once I ended up back at the bar. In Algoma at night, the bar seemed to be the only place one could go to socialize but I instinctively knew the kind of women that came there were not the ones I wanted to marry. I somehow put two and two together and realized I had no future in drinking establishments.

So instead of the bar on summer nights to deal with my loneliness, I rode my bicycle around Algoma. Being a small town, it doesn't take long to ride every street. Then I would head up to my apartment. But when I got there, and the loneliness would surround me again, I would go back down and ride some more. One time, I drove my car around Algoma so many times that the Algoma policeman actually called me on the CB radio and asked me if he could help me find the place I was looking for. It takes even less time to drive all the streets of Algoma than it does to bike around them, but because I couldn't make myself park my car and go up into that den of loneliness, I just kept driving.

I have a pistol and I kept it by my bed. I purposely kept it unloaded in the hopes that by the time I got it loaded to kill myself, I would have thought it through more. Then I went out and bought a speed loader for the pistol. Loneliness was always there during that time. I started to go to the ball park in Algoma after the ball games were over and lay in the middle of the field in the dark, looking at the stars. In Psalms 19:1 David said, "The heavens declare the glory of God and the firmament showeth his handiwork." At that time in my life, I am afraid all the heavens did for me was make me feel even smaller and lonelier. One time when I was so lonely, I even walked the railroad tracks from Algoma to Pulaski at midnight, a distance of about fifteen miles round trip.

As the old Lutheran church of Algoma was by the ballpark, I would sometimes sit on its hard, cold concrete steps wondering why the Pastor or someone else didn't know how I felt, yet I hadn't told anyone. I did start to write my feelings in a journal and I believe that helped. Even now if I go back and read what I had written, those feelings of loneliness are very real. More than once, I picked up my Bible after loading the pistol and read Matthew 28:20, which says, "and lo I am with you always." At that point in my life, it didn't seem to help much.

I had all along been going to the church of my youth, mostly I believe, because it was expected of me. Then one night as I sat on the steps of that church, I prayed and asked Jesus into my heart. I told Him I was a sinner and I needed Him. I wish I could say some big change occurred, but it didn't right away. Yet not long after, I realized I was going to church to worship Jesus, not because it was expected of me. All my life I had thought I was a Christian yet on that calm starry night, I became a true Christian. Like most important things in my life, I didn't realize how much that little act would change my life. I don't even remember the day or the year. It was probably a year after before I actually realized what had happened then.

My personality seems to be such that I need big pushes to move me into new areas. I ended up going to electrical trade school because my brother wanted to farm more than I did, and I needed to do something. I moved away from my parents' home only because my boss insisted I needed to be closer to Algoma to take service calls. I bought my first place (the apartment & shop in Algoma) because my boss thought it would be a good place for me and subsequently, I started my electrical business because my boss wished to get out of it and didn't need me anymore. I got that same kind of shove into marriage because Amanda gave me an ultimatum. And finally, I live in a nice new house because my wife provided the motivation and drive to build it. I guess what I'm trying to say is Jesus used my great loneliness to push me towards accepting His call for my life. I am sure that God was working in my life before I accepted Him, but I can more easily see His work in my life since that time.

Sometime after this (at 33 years of age), a friend from church set me up on a blind date. The lady was pretty and nice yet unsure of her direction. After we dated about six months, she told me she just wanted to be friends and wasn't interested in marriage. I guess I wasn't too subtle in my intentions, as I was interested in marriage. I realized that I really liked the company and this relationship spurred me into seeking companionship. I placed a personal ad in the Superior newspaper. Before I did, I told myself I would take anyone out to lunch that answered my ad. This was back before the electronic age when all correspondence was done by letters through a Post Bulletin box number. I ended up dating six or seven different women with nothing coming of any of those dates. I answered some ads also and that is how I met my wife. I almost didn't answer the ad she placed. . .

In fact, I went back and dug the ad out of the garbage to answer it. I had looked at it and thought it was interesting, but I thought she was very specific in what she was looking for and I didn't think I fit. Twelve years later, I'm still not sure I fit the bill. I wrote my letter and went on with my life. She told me later that before contacting me, she did some research. She had my phone number from my letter, so she looked through the Algoma phone book until she found my number and then she knew my name and what I did. She asked around at the hospital where she worked to see if anyone knew me. She actually found someone who went to church with me and I guess I got rave reviews. Satisfied with what she found out, she called me. God got me to my apartment office to answer that call at just the right time. I was never home from work at 4 p.m. on a Friday afternoon, but I had just stopped to do a quick task I needed to do there - two minutes at most. Amanda, my wife now, said she wouldn't have tried again if I hadn't answered. You see, she wasn't really looking. She was happy where she was and had placed the ad on a lark to see what responses she would get.

Now I have to be honest. That phone call scared me to death as she told me she was Mennonite and that she wore long plain dresses and a white cap on her head. That was how I would recognize her when we met for lunch. I wanted nothing to do with the Mennonites. I surely wasn't going to change and become one. But I had promised myself I would take any ladies who contacted me out to lunch. I figured this was going to be the fastest lunch I ever did eat, in and out - promise kept. God had other plans. We talked and found a lot in common. We even spent the whole afternoon walking and talking at a county park about five miles from Superior. We dated for a while and then one day she said, "I will give you another year to decide if you want to marry me or not. I am not going to mess around wishy washy for years." It was the push I needed. We were married Sept 14, 1991. I was thirty-six years old.

I believe God gave me the loneliness, so I could truly appreciate the Godly woman He gave me as a mate. It, of course, took me about a year to really realize that I was actually married. We meshed together so well that it seemed like we had been married forever. When I today see all God did to get us together, I am awed and know without Him, we would not have gotten together. God has also given me a great daughter and gotten Amanda and I through her cancer seven years ago now. He has given me the strength to be up here talking to you today.

Before I met Amanda, I started praying for someone to be my friend, my wife, my lover, and the mother of my children - in that order please, God. In Amanda, I got just that and, in that order, too. We have this joke between us. I do most of the cooking at our house because Amanda doesn't like to. It's not her fault after all. I didn't pray for someone who could cook. God gave me exactly what I prayed for. Anyway, I don't mind cooking. It beats loneliness.

The last three years have been a time of stretching and growing in my faith and my relationships. I don't know why God has put me here in this church at this time, but I have done things in the last two years that only God could have gotten me to do. He gave me that push into being your Elder Board Chairman when the position was vacated by the moving away of the previous chairman in midyear. Then Pastor Frank resigned, and I found myself needing to grow in many ways to meet the needs of the church body. Being up here today is another big step of faith. Three short years ago, none of this would have happened if I had had the choice to make.

I hope somehow this little talk will help you get closer to your caboose. I want to thank you all for helping me get my caboose closer to my engine also. I would ask that God bless you all with all the blessings of His kingdom and give you the peace found only in the knowledge of knowing Jesus.

At the beginning of this little speech, I told you I would leave you with a little something to think about. So here it is. In Psalms

46:10, it says, "Be still and know that I am God." I ask you to take two minutes sometime this next week and be still. Instead of counting your blessings, count all the sins that you personally heaped onto Jesus on that cross. If you do it honestly, as I have, you will see how much Jesus really did for you on that cross and it will remind you of the wonder and the joy of having this freight removed from the train of your life. Just something to think about. Thank you very much.

Chapter 5 The Coming of a New Pastor

The church, as a whole, is truly low and discouraged. When one gets to the point where he realizes he can't fix anything by himself, he does what he should have been doing all along. He prays and asks God for help. So, the search committee and the church pray earnestly and keep on being a church the best that they can. Meanwhile, the pastor search committee struggles to find the candidate that will best meet the needs of this church. All the members know what they want but don't believe in their hearts that any of us are good enough for God to give us that top notch man. The committee members go through many interviews but can't seem to find that right fit. They pray. The church prays some more. The search committee has looked at all the applications that have been received. Then a last-minute application comes in. The package seems too good to be true. This man has charisma, a humbleness about him, a love for the Lord, excellent sermon presentation skills, and enthusiasm. Everyone is excited. We need to hire this man before he goes somewhere else. By mid-June, Pastor Travis and Susan with baby girl come to be our ministerial team. We are a functioning thriving church again.

During this time without a pastor, Gordon, as Chairman of the Board, has taken the reigns of the leadership of the church. He goes off the elder board at the beginning of 2002 but continues on the Search Committee for another six months. And with the coming of the new pastor in June, his commitments at church all but disappear. As the treasurer, I have taken over the responsibilities of managing the office, making sure the bulletins are printed, the bills paid, the copier repaired, and numerous other tasks to keep the physical side of the church operating smoothly. We have highly invested ourselves and taken ownership in this church. This will prove, I believe, to be one of the factors in our downfall later.

But for now, we are poised at the top of the rollercoaster. Gordon switches his efforts to wiring the new house of the pastor being built by one of the contractors in the congregation. In his woodworking shop, he builds a cross for the front of the church. And he spends hours again in decorating for Vacation Bible School. This year's theme is camping. This calls for erecting tents, making cardboard mountain lions, and creating an authentic camping experience for the children. He seems to be doing well emotionally with the transition from the role of leader to that of a follower of the new pastor.

∞∞∞∞

All the members of the Administrative Council are gathered for a meeting. I remain the treasurer of the church, a position that has given me a voice in the affairs of the church and the respect of the other board members. Pastor Travis has joined us as he settles into his new job. The discussion eventually turns towards sharing ideas on how to revitalize the church.

"We want to be known as a praying church." Travis emphasizes, "I would like to start having a prayer meeting on Sunday evenings."

"I just want to bring to your attention that people like to have Sunday evenings to be with their families," I respond back.

"If people really loved the Lord then prayer meeting would come first regardless of which day of the week it is," he shoots back.

I quickly withdraw into myself and go silent. I am hurt at the insinuation that wanting to be with family is not acceptable and labels one as not truly dedicated to the Lord. Tears slip out the corners of my eyes and I know it is time to leave. I gather my books and walk out the door. Aware that his words have changed the tone of the meeting, he follows me.

"I am so sorry that I offended you. I need to be more sensitive to those I am working with in leadership. Will you forgive me?"

I am truly touched by his humility and depth of perception. "Of course, I will forgive you."

A few weeks later, I send him an e-mail,

I just wanted you to know too that I believe you and Susan are a gift from God to our church and we (Gordon, I, and the rest of the church) want to support you in any way we can. I am sure you know this but sometimes when the going gets tough, one needs to hear those words. I will pray that God will give you and the elders the wisdom to discern the truth and the courage to respond to it in the way God leads. I also pray that you will be a man of integrity and high character throughout your years as a pastor and that you not grow weary and faint by the way; that the devil will not be able to cause you to fall and thus malign the name of Christ. Being a pastor has to be one of the toughest jobs there are as it requires much emotionally, physically, and spiritually. May the Lord sustain you daily. Amanda

Travis responds with the same graciousness, "Thanks for your words of encouragement. We need the prayers that you are praying for us. I am grateful to serve alongside of you and Gordon." The humility on the part of both parties has caused the early clash to be put behind us.

∞∞∞∞

Gordon and I stand together on the pulpit platform on our twelfth wedding anniversary as Pastor Travis blesses us before the congregation. Our purpose is to recommit to each other by signing a marriage covenant before our friends and church family. In April, Gordon and I had taken some time off to attend a Marriage to Remember conference in the cities put on by Family Life and sponsored by this church. We liked the idea of signing a marriage covenant as a statement to one's children and the world that we intended to stay together forever. Erin and our new beloved Pastor Travis sign this covenant with us.

∞∞∞∞

The year 2003, Pastor Travis's first full year at Truth goes extremely well. The church has again become vibrant under this new leadership. A young man, Kyle, who has been involved in the youth group is offered a salary to take on a part-time youth leader position, a position the church has not had until now. There is talk again of building an addition onto the church as the church was able to pay off the existing building mortgage at the end of 2002. They did this by combining savings and the annual November Harvest Dinner offering. In anticipation of this addition, a

Building Task Force is appointed. Being familiar with the construction trades, Gordon is included on this task force. He draws a simple design of how he sees the addition looking and works up an electrical proposal to estimate the cost of the electrical.

As the treasurer, I am extremely busy in coordinating the buying of many new needed supplies as the church gears up for innovative and exciting ministries under new leadership. A new computer, new cabinets, and a new countertop are installed in the office. All of these purchases are approved by the Administrative Council but there is little opposition to the decisions that I make regarding the purchases. I am consulted by the Elder Board for input into the pastor's salary and depended on to develop a budget that I present to the Elder Board and Administrative Council for 2003. I feel valued, respected, and a crucial member of the team. Hierarchy plays little role in the functioning of the leadership but instead everyone's input is accepted as of equal value. Communication is open and frequent between volunteers and leaders.

Vacation Bible School in July has become a fun and anticipated time of year. This year, the children begin their journey through a barn built around cardboard cows. Kids sing and study the word of God around a field of cornstalks in the middle of the church. A scarecrow waves from the cornfield. As if he didn't have enough to do already, Gordon has found his creativity in developing these themes for VBS. Even the Sunday morning service before the start of VBS needs to be varied to accommodate the crops and cows that take up the sanctuary.

Chapter 6 Smooth Sailing in Pastor Travis's Ministry with a Preemptory Blip

O n July 18, 2004 just two years into his pastorate, Pastor Travis preaches a sermon that will blow us away. He chooses the text *Ephesians 2:4*

"For he chose us in him before the creation of the world to be holy and blameless in his sight. In love, he predestined us to be adopted as his sons through Jesus Christ, in accordance with his pleasure and will..." Before God created anything; the universe, time, or existence, he determined to set his love upon you, determined to rescue you from the sin he knew you would commit. God is sovereignly saving according to his choosing. He was so specific in choosing you, he made a record of it before time began. In fact, in Revelations 13, He says that your name has or has not been written in the book of life before time began.

Gordon and I go home from church in a turmoil. What just happened? I sit down and do what is my standard method of responding to confusing circumstance. I write an e-mail to Pastor Travis.

I love your charisma, your enthusiasm, and your strong leadership of Truth and don't wish to discourage you in any way, but I was somewhat distressed and confused by your message on "election" on Sunday. I am not a Biblical scholar by any means and I hope you can be gracious towards my thoughts. In spite of trying to balance what you had to say with various scriptures, it still sounded to me a lot like only certain people are elected and called to be saved and God chose who they would be a long time ago. Essentially then, the purpose of witnessing to others is so that maybe one will eventually witness to those who have already been chosen and close the gap for them and the others are a lost cause anyway. When all scriptures are considered, I do not believe that is what the Bible is saying. I haven't seen you live your walk of faith that way either, so I am hoping that I am just not understanding correctly what you were saying. I am especially concerned for those in the church who are newer in the faith or not well grounded becoming confused and losing faith. One of your points was that this doctrine should be a comfort to us. I was not at all comforted but troubled. Even knowing in my heart and soul that the message of salvation is open to all and that I am one of his, the doubt of "maybe I'm not one of the chosen predestinated ones" crept into my mind and threatened to rattle my faith. The question of whether salvation is open to all is a basic tenet of my faith and effects all the rest of my beliefs and behaviors, so I guess that's why I find it important to address. Thank you for your time and graciousness.

I explain in another e-mail my interpretation and what has always been my understanding of this verse:

I guess I am not having problems with my assurance of salvation unless one begins to say that we are predestined (as in the sense of "it's all preplanned and determined for each one from the beginning of time" and we have no choice in the matter) to accept God's plan of salvation or not. That is what I was hearing and that is where the problem comes in. I don't read Ephesians 1:4 to mean that it was planned WHO would be saved but that for those who do choose to follow him, it was planned before time began that they would be holy and blameless and be accepted as adopted sons. In the NIV Romans 8:29 says, "For whom he did foreknow, he also did predestinate to be conformed to the image of his son." This predestination has nothing to do with who will be saved either but is a statement that he who believes is predestined to become like His son Jesus.

∞∞∞∞

Vacation Bible School starts the week after this message. Gordon has again put in many hours decorating for this time of outreach. But we have little enthusiasm for this year. We sit together on the green grass of the bank in front of the church and disconnectedly gaze at the children running and playing in the field. Our hearts are in turmoil and we are lost in our confusion and uncertainty. How can we stay in a church that does not hold the same beliefs that we do? How can we leave a church where we have become so established? What are we going to do? What should we do? Erin is eleven years old. Do we want to tear her away from the church where her friends are at a very crucial time in her life? We love Pastor Travis too and have become close friends. How did we miss this when hiring him?

Pastor Travis is gracious and kind throughout this time of questioning. He reassures us, "it is okay if in the final analysis we have a differing perspective on this matter. The main thing is that we do our best to bring to bear the whole council of God on this matter... It's okay to struggle with what the Bible says about election, and you don't need to feel guilty about being uncomfortable with it. I have been there. I will not insist that everyone agrees with me on every point regarding these matters. Many people have overemphasized this doctrine. I don't plan to do that."

These words we find comforting. Though we still don't know what to do, as we watch closely over the coming weeks, we hear nothing more about predestination and begin to relax. *Maybe he has realized his mistake.* In August, I resign my treasurer's position so that I might return to school full time to become a nurse anesthetist. This opens the way for Gordon to take over as Chairman of the Administrative Council. The treasurer's role is taken up by Samuel, a gentleman who is a banker by trade. It seems like we are back on track.

This theological issue takes a total back seat when in October, the youth pastor is discovered unclothed with one of the young girls in his office. The church is thrown into a far more commanding crisis of sexual abuse which the senior pastor and leadership must respond to. The youth group is hurled into confusion with this turn of events. The youth loved their pastor and had just put on the biggest youth event that the church had ever hosted. Truckloads of sand were dumped on the church lawn and the area turned into a beach party with concert music. Gordon had been involved in chaperoning the event and in setting up the power needed for this huge event. An exhilarating experience on top of the mountain quickly cascades into a tumbling somersault to the bottom of the valley. The whole church is in shock especially those families who have teenagers in the youth group. A lot of energy and focus is turned towards responding to this embarrassing situation in this small community. Just when we thought we were turning the reputation of the church around in the community, this happens. For ourselves, we are thankful that our daughter is not yet youth group age and seems to be somewhat shielded from the faith crisis this turn of events triggers for many of the youth.

"God has shepherded us through some very difficult times, including the painful days of dismissing our youth pastor," are the words of Pastor Travis at the annual meeting that year.[8] An interim youth pastor is brought in who has counseling experience in such situations to help move the youth through this perplexing time and to help them process what has happened.

In spite of this shattering incident, joy and blessing are found in a different choice by others in the congregation. "Without question, one of the greatest highlights of 2004 was to see the beginning progress towards planting a church in the Ephesus area, a town about twenty miles from Corinth. What a joyous celebration we had on November 14 as we surprised our Ephesus families by giving them a $20,000 grant for the new church plant."[8] It had been suggested to the board that the Ephesus Area was in need of a Bible-believing church. Many in attendance had been driving from Ephesus to Truth. After much prayer and consideration, a decision was made to halt plans on the addition to the Corinth church and to launch a church plant in Ephesus.

∞∞∞∞

2005 is a year for the church spent "dealing with the healing process that was needed as a result of actions from the previous year. Unfortunately, while necessary, it took away time needed for other matters," so reads the end of year report. Also, as a result of the unfortunate happenings of the prior year, the Christian Education team is charged with drawing up a rough draft of a Sexual Abuse Policy. And an associate pastor search team is put together to replace the departed disgraced youth pastor.

In July, Gordon takes a week off and does something he hasn't done since we are married. He takes a trip to Kentucky to help with the building of the Creation Museum being constructed there by Answers In Genesis. In the last few years, he has had an interest in creation evangelism and decided to donate his services to promote creationism as taught in the Bible. He is especially interested in exploring the scientific and technical aspects of various elements of the Creator's intelligent design and His planning as evidenced in the ark dimensions needed for the worldwide flood written about in Genesis.

When he returns, it is soon time to set up for Vacation Bible School. This year sports an African theme. In the middle of the church grows a fourteen-foot umbrella thorn savanna tree. A twelve-foot mama giraffe reaches up into the high ceiling. She is followed around by a baby giraffe. Close by rests a zebra and her baby. From the lights swing cardboard monkeys. And in the blue water hole, hippo heads peak out. The smiles on the faces of the children are enough thanks for my hubby who enjoys using his creative talents.

Gordon continues to support the ongoing efforts of the church through his leadership of the Administrative Council. Erin is in her last year of AWANA before moving into the youth group. And I am somewhat removed from church activities this year as I turn most of my time towards my studies. But in spite of that, together, Gordon and I, attend most of the prayer meetings held at the church. Though the group of people who faithfully come together to pray is small, we are committed to supporting our pastor in this especially important activity. Gordon feels strongly that we cannot let another pastor labor in prayer alone. Pastor Travis is sometimes discouraged and perplexed as to why more people do not come to prayer meeting. He has a vision of a vital praying church. We are committed to kneeling with him.

∞∞∞∞

2006 offers little change from the prior year. We are happy with our church and often invite people to come and become a part of us.

Gordon continues to enjoy his part in the decorating for Vacation Bible School. In 2006, a large ship rises out of the floor. It is stranded on a sandy beach in the middle of the church. Gordon crafts a beautiful wooden treasure chest that he fills with fake gold and silver coins. The treasure, of course, is Jesus. The kids love climbing on the ship and eating their snack there during a break in the action.

The Sunday School curriculum, as well as the VBS curriculum, continues to be purchased from Gospel Light Publisher. Gospel Light is a non-denominational publisher and according to their website states that their Sunday school lessons "lead kids to Jesus." They are considered evangelical and their statement of beliefs include stating that the Bible is "the Divinely inspired and authoritative Word of God, the only infallible rule of faith and practice."[9] There is no indication of any beliefs being taught that would be different from our ingrained, deep-rooted understanding of the Word of God.

The Christian Education Team is restructured this year to include only ministry leaders such as AWANA, Sunday School Superintendent, Children's Church Coordinator, and the Youth Group leader. It has been two years since the sexual abuse scandal and emotions have settled down somewhat. There is continued work on a child protection policy to try to prevent any future disturbing behavior, but the interim youth pastor feels that his work is complete and leaves the staff. A young lady whom I will call Kathy steps unofficially into the role of youth group leader. She grew up with the youth group and has been involved for some time in a leadership role. I think she would be a good choice. I write a letter to the elder board in early 2007 in support of hiring her as the new interim until a permanent youth pastor can be found.

Dear Elders: People feel that Kathy is the ideal candidate for the job. I don't know what has been talked about at elder meetings or if she has been approached. I keep getting the feeling from Kathy, though, that she is in limbo but might consider staying here if she had affordable housing and an adequate income. I know $6,000 was put in the church budget for such a position... I just feel we are allowing the person God would have in this job slip away because of financial support. If we can't pay someone $15,000 - $20,000 per year temporarily until we can obtain a youth pastor, there is no way we can pay a youth pastor $50,000-$60,000... I just feel strongly that this is the answer to our prayer for the youth right now. Thanks for listening.

Having a woman in a leadership position such as this has never been done at this church, but I don't see a problem. The official stance of the congregation is to have only men in the top leadership positions such as pastor and elder, but women have always been welcomed and encouraged to fill any other positions. This is evidenced by the fact that the elder board does approve and hire Kathy shortly after this as the interim youth pastor.

Erin graduates into the youth group this year, 2007, under Kathy's leadership. Erin also transitions into being a leader on Wednesday evenings for the younger kids in AWANA. AWANA has been a hugely successful program for the children, drawing many kids from the community who are not a part of this particular church. AWANA (derived from the first letters of "Approved Workmen Are Not Ashamed" as taken from 2 Timothy 2:15) is an international evangelical Christian nonprofit organization founded in 1950, headquartered in Streamwood, Illinois. The mission of AWANA is to help "reach kids, equip leaders and change the world for God."[10] There is a large emphasis on scripture memorization, but also times for snacks and games. It is a growing ministry in the church.

∞∞∞∞

Gordon gathers up his tools after another evening of work at the church. He is busy constructing a raised sound booth for the back of the church. Into the side of that, he builds bookshelves for the library, and underneath is a large storage area for the foldable tables and extra chairs that can be pulled out for fellowship meals and events. This is the solution that the Administrative Council has come up with to solve three different problems; the need for more library space, the need for more storage, and a safe place to keep the sound board and overhead projector/computer protected from the flying objects in the hands of children at play. Gordon is always at the ready to lend his hand to the needs of the church.

Privately by 2007, I am consumed by the hurt and rejection of my family of origin and find myself focused on it. I force myself to attend a Freedom in Christ conference

(Anderson 2004) that is being held at the church in October. One of the sessions of the conference focuses on forgiving those who have hurt you. The message is that forgiveness will set you free. But what really is forgiveness, I ask? The answer I receive is that it is "cancelling the debt" regardless of the other person's response. Every attendee is walked through saying the words for all those people who have offended them. Just saying the words, for me, does not fix anything. It all sounds so trite and simplistic.

Many times over the years, I share my struggles with my family of origin with Pastor Travis and others in the church and seek their council. The desire to be loved and accepted as part of the family and to be treated as a daughter and sister exerts a powerful pull. I do not know how to forgive and move on from the drama and chaos that always seems to engulf my family. Therefore, this little church congregation has become my family and the shelter in the midst of the storms that always seems to swirl around my household of origin.

Chapter 7 The Simple Message of Salvation Proclaimed

2007 closes for the church with Gordon again preaching a sermon at the end of the first week of December to allow Pastor Travis to celebrate the birth of his last child and first son.

I have entitled this little speech, "Lower than a snake's belly in a wagon rut." I got that from that great Bible teaching TV show, "The Beverly Hillbillies." Maybe some of you remember that show. I think that "lower than a snake's belly in a wagon rut" is a very descriptive statement. Can't you just see a snake in a deep wagon rut in a low valley? That's about as low as one can get without going underground. This state of affairs might describe a person or an organization such as a church. Could we also say it might describe how God himself felt before he destroyed the world with a flood?

In Genesis 6:5-7 it says, "And God saw that the wickedness of man was great in the earth, and that every imagination of the thoughts of his heart was only evil continually and it repented the Lord that He had made man on the earth, and it grieved Him at His heart. And the Lord said, I will destroy man whom I have created from the face of the earth. Both man, and beast, and the creeping thing and the fowls of the air: for it repenteth me that I have made them."

That sounds like God was feeling very "discouraged" and low over the actions of his own special creation that he created with love in His own image and had blessed. In Genesis 1:27, it says, "God created man in His own image. In the image of God created He him..." In verse 28, it says, "and God blessed them..." and in verse 31, it says, "God saw everything that He had made and behold, it was very good."

If you, as a parent, "created" a child in your image, loved it, blessed it, and saw that it was a beautiful creation and then he or she did only evil continuously, it would grieve your heart to the core and probably leave you feeling "lower than a snake's belly in a wagon rut."

Even though it seemed God was at His lowest point in regards to his creation, in Genesis 6:8, it says, "but Noah found grace in the eyes of the Lord." The righteousness of one man led to the saving of the human race and God's promise to never totally cover the earth with water again.

Since it is the Christmas season, let us look at an event that is much on our minds these days. Were the days leading up to Jesus birth a happy time? I would guess that Joseph and Mary experienced some of the lowest, most difficult times in their lives before that birth in Bethlehem. In Luke 2: 3-5, it says, "and all went to be taxed, everyone into his own city. And Joseph also went up from Galilee, out of the city of Nazareth, into Judea, into the city of David, which is called Bethlehem to be taxed with Mary, his espoused wife, being great with child.

A hundred miles of walking for Joseph? Leading a donkey, with a very pregnant wife? And to top it off, the reason they were doing this traveling was because of taxes and the oppression of the Roman government. And, of course, the last straw is they can't find a place to stay. Joseph may have gotten wagon rut low on the way to Bethlehem both spiritually and in reality. I can imagine that the roads of Israel were often full of deep ruts that made travel difficult. However, as you all know, God had not forgotten them. He had a place planned for them to stay and a healthy baby Jesus was born. That very special baby, Jesus, was born in some very difficult circumstances. His birth, though, fulfilled the promise God had made that he would come to man.

Now, the way I see it, the lowest low experienced by anyone in the Bible must have happened to Jesus himself as he hung on the cross.

In Matthew 21:9, we find "and the multitudes that went before and that followed, cried, saying Hosanna to the Son of David: Blessed is He that cometh in the name of the lord." This is a snapshot of Jesus' triumphant entry into Jerusalem. In Luke, it says that the rocks would cry out if the multitudes didn't. Not long after that high in Jesus life, in Matthew 27:26, it says "when he had scourged Jesus, he delivered Him to be crucified."

Going from the multitudes praising Him and hailing Him as king to a whipping and being sentenced to death on the cross must have been a "wagon rut" experience, I would think. However, the worst is yet to come for Jesus. Just listen to Matthew 27:46, "and about the ninth hour Jesus cried with a loud voice, saying, My God, my God, why hast thou forsaken me." Here the Son of God, who has had an eternal relationship with the Father, has that relationship interrupted while hanging on a wooden cross with the sins of all mankind on his back. I would think that would be a "lower than a snake's belly in a wagon rut" experience.

Yet in a little while Jesus is resurrected from the dead and through His sacrifice, the plan of salvation for all men is completed. In Mark 16:19, it says, "He was received up into Heaven, and sits on the right hand of God."

Chapter 8 Subtle Changes

After much prayer, Gordon says "yes" to having his name placed on the ballot for elder again in 2008. He is elected at the annual meeting in January for a term of four years. This requires him to relinquish his position as the Administrative Council Chairman. Also, at the annual meeting, Pastor Travis informs the congregation that the EFCA has updated its Statement of Faith. He tells us that nothing has changed in the basic beliefs and the Free Church maintains the "unity in essentials, charity in non-essentials" position that it has always held. Without any further discussion, a motion is made to accept the new statement and the congregation unanimously accepts the new version as their own.

According to Adam Talbott, an Evangelical Free pastor, on his blog in 2008,

The 2008 statement continues keeping the door open to all who affirm solid Bible doctrine. To be more specific, the framers of the 1950 Statement were almost entirely Arminian Dispensationalists, but many pastors and Trinity Divinity professors from a Reformed perspective are now serving throughout the denomination. The new Statement removes the previous Arminian and Dispensational bias... In my best judgement, the new statement protects the EFCA from modern theological controversies and it also broadens the fellowship of the EFCA to include some of us from a "reformed" theological position.

This intent and change in the EFCA Statement of Faith is not communicated to us nor discussed with the congregation. But it will have a huge impact on the direction of Truth Evangelical Free Church and our personal lives.

Being on the elder board always seems to require an enormous number of hours for a lay person who also has another occupation. There are expectations for attendance every Sunday evening at an elder Bible study. Pastor Travis is having the elders work through a Bible Study called "The Word" published by the Center for Church Based Training. The study looks at systematic theology as it relates to the church with the goal of helping "local church leaders clarify their own theological beliefs in aspects of core orthodox Christian doctrines."[11] A secondary resource being used is a book by Wayne Grudem titled *Systematic Theology: An Introduction to Biblical Doctrine.* Gordon has a simple faith, so it does not even occur to him that this study is based on a position different than the one he has always ascribed to. He has moments when it crosses his mind that some points that are being taught are not what he believes. In looking back, the study is definitely Calvinistic based, but the learners are never informed of this and there is nothing blatant in the text identifying it as such. Gordon loves Pastor Travis. He is warm, friendly, and kind. His personality draws people to him and people follow him. It never occurs to Gordon that Pastor Travis is teaching from a different systematic theology than he would subscribe to. He trusts Pastor Travis implicitly.

EFCA Statement of Faith
Adopted by the Conference on June 26, 2008

The Evangelical Free Church of America is an association of autonomous churches united around these theological convictions:

God

1. We believe in one God, Creator of all things, holy, infinitely perfect, and eternally existing in a loving unity of three equally divine Persons: the Father, the Son and the Holy Spirit. Having limitless knowledge and sovereign power, God has graciously purposed from eternity to redeem a people for Himself and to make all things new for His own glory.

The Bible

2. We believe that God has spoken in the Scriptures, both Old and New Testaments, through the words of human authors. As the verbally inspired Word of God, the Bible is without error in the original writings, the complete revelation of His will for salvation, and the ultimate authority by which every realm of human knowledge and endeavor should be judged. Therefore, it is to be believed in all that it teaches, obeyed in all that it requires, and trusted in all that it promises.

The Human Condition

3. We believe that God created Adam and Eve in His image, but they sinned when tempted by Satan. In union with Adam, human beings are sinners by nature and by choice, alienated from God, and under His wrath. Only through God's saving work in Jesus Christ can we be rescued, reconciled and renewed.

Jesus Christ

4. We believe that Jesus Christ is God incarnate, fully God and fully man, one Person in two natures. Jesus—Israel's promised Messiah—was conceived through the Holy Spirit and born of the virgin Mary. He lived a sinless life, was crucified under Pontius Pilate, arose bodily from the dead, ascended into heaven and sits at the right hand of God the Father as our High Priest and Advocate.

The Work of Christ

5. We believe that Jesus Christ, as our representative and substitute, shed His blood on the cross as the perfect, all-sufficient sacrifice for our sins. His atoning death and victorious resurrection constitute the only ground for salvation.

The Holy Spirit

6. We believe that the Holy Spirit, in all that He does, glorifies the Lord Jesus Christ. He convicts the world of its guilt. He regenerates sinners, and in Him they are baptized into union with Christ and adopted as heirs in the family of God. He also indwells, illuminates, guides, equips and empowers believers for Christ-like living and service.

The Church

7. We believe that the true church comprises all who have been justified by God's grace through faith alone in Christ alone. They are united by the Holy Spirit in the body of Christ, of which He is the Head. The true church is manifest in local churches, whose membership should be composed only of believers. The Lord Jesus mandated two ordinances, baptism and the Lord's Supper, which visibly and tangibly express the gospel. Though they are not the means of salvation, when celebrated by the church in

genuine faith, these ordinances confirm and nourish the believer.

Christian Living

8. We believe that God's justifying grace must not be separated from His sanctifying power and purpose. God commands us to love Him supremely and others sacrificially, and to live out our faith with care for one another, compassion toward the poor and justice for the oppressed. With God's Word, the Spirit's power, and fervent prayer in Christ's name, we are to combat the spiritual forces of evil. In obedience to Christ's commission, we are to make disciples among all people, always bearing witness to the gospel in word and deed.

Christ's Return

9. We believe in the personal, bodily and premillennial return of our Lord Jesus Christ. The coming of Christ, at a time known only to God, demands constant expectancy and, as our blessed hope, motivates the believer to godly living, sacrificial service and energetic mission.

Response and Eternal Destiny

10. We believe that God commands everyone everywhere to believe the gospel by turning to Him in repentance and receiving the Lord Jesus Christ. We believe that God will raise the dead bodily and judge the world, assigning the unbeliever to condemnation and eternal conscious punishment and the believer to eternal blessedness and joy with the Lord in the new heaven and the new earth, to the praise of His glorious grace. Amen.

Copied from the EFCA website

https://go.efca.org/sites/default/files/resources/docs/2014/05/efca_statement_of_faith_6-26-08.pdf

We have long forgotten the predestination sermon. It isn't until later that we realize we have been blind and in denial because it never occurs to us that Pastor Travis is systematically changing the basic theological position of Truth Evangelical Free church.

There is also a general elder meeting once per month. Some of these meetings run well into the night. But one tries to rationalize that it is an honor to serve and to not allow one's own expectations to interfere with the commitment to the church. The biggest decision made by the board this year is to add an administrative assistant to the payroll. This position will provide support to both pastors once a new associate pastor can be hired.

∞∞∞∞

This summer for Vacation Bible School, Gordon spends several months on his most aggressive woodworking project yet. The VBS leader commented that she would love to have a working rollercoaster for the year's VBS (not really expecting that he would build one). So in our horse pasture behind the barn there slowly sprouts a wooden rollercoaster. My brother and his wife, from Virginia, decide to come for a visit as Gordon is making the final touches on the rollercoaster. My brother, being a brave and trusting soul, volunteers to make the virgin test run. Everything goes well until the next to the last curve at the bottom of the hill. The little roller coaster car, with my brother inside, is going a little too fast and dumps off the curve. It is obvious that there is a need for some redesign on the engineering end. After making some changes, my brother's next ride is uneventful.

Gordon hires the two men that work for him to take down the roller coaster and reassemble it in the church on the Friday before VBS instead of doing electrical work. VBS is a huge success drawing approximately one hundred kids each night for the five nights. What results is a not-very-controlled chaos as the VBS organizers are not prepared for the large crowd. Each child is given the opportunity to ride once a night. Thank the Lord, the car stays on the track and no one falls out or is injured. All the youth and adult leaders including the pastor get after-hour rides.

∞∞∞∞

The year of 2009 brings a new associate pastor to Truth. I will call him Pastor Jack. Kathy who has served as the youth leader for a couple of years moves on. The administrative assistant position approved by the elder board last year is filled by Pastor Jack's wife, Jill. Together, the new couple becomes a huge asset to the church. We are happy with our friendly church. It seems healthy. It is welcoming. We often invite people to come to our church and try it out.

With the arrival of Pastor Jack, many new ventures are commenced with the help of a newly selected Outreach Team. A summer block party is organized in the mobile home park which has a high percentage of Hispanic migrant workers. The intention is to reach out to this population through caring and casual contact. A grocery give-away is planned at Thanksgiving time to bless those in need in the community. Groceries, Bibles, and tracts are given to those struggling to make ends meet. And a Faith Works Partnership is begun with the local school district to provide some very needed painting in the school buildings. The church seems to be vibrant and growing.

Chapter 9 A Return to A Leadership Role

I have been done with anesthesia school for a couple of years now. Samuel, the banker who took over the treasurer position when I went back to school, is now ready for a break. I step back into the treasurer role on the Administrative Council at the beginning of 2010. I look forward to contributing to the decision-making process of the church again. I watched how Samuel was treated with respect and honor, invited to the elder budget meeting to advise the elders on the pastors' salaries and allowed to make everyday decisions about the distribution of funds to various ministries. I have an expectation of being allowed to do these things too in the same position as I had done before I left.

I have always been an outspoken person and not afraid to freely speak my mind. In years past, others have listened to me respectfully as the treasurer, so it isn't long before I begin to express my opinions about various issues. I write an open letter to the leadership in May 2010 in regard to plans to remove the windows in the front of the sanctuary in preparation for video recording of the sermons for broadcasting.

The suggestion was made on Sunday that we put our thoughts and recommendations on paper to the building committee in regards to the windows. I am not sure what I want to write but I am concerned about the various building projects we are contemplating. First, I am OK with spending money to maintain the condition of the current building (ie new roof, siding replacement, painting etc). I do have a concern, though, that some of the other building changes do not seem to have a long-range plan in mind. To me, it is not whether we take windows out or not or whether we do a major renovation of the foyer, but what is it exactly that we are attempting to accomplish? Do we have any intention of building a new sanctuary in the foreseeable future? What criteria need to be met before we determine that God is leading us in that direction? Does everyone need to be tithing and the church meeting budget every week? If that is what we are looking for, what do we do about the overflowing seating from the influx of new people - the fruit God is providing? If we have extra money, does that mean we should be spending it now? Maybe we should be saving as much every month as we can for a building later. I am just throwing out thoughts as I don't have the answers. My mantra always is, "If it isn't broken, don't try to fix it." Save the money that could be spent for the bigger goal (assuming we have one).

Specifically, regarding the windows up front, I like them the way they are. Someone had a reason for making it that way in the beginning and this issue has been there from the beginning. Do we really need to spend money to make a change at this particular point in time? I do understand that it was brought up now because of the need to change the windows anyway. We did agree to get them tinted and I assume we will still cover them with material. I think the upper windows need to be tinted more though. If we really must make a change, I can live with removing the bottom windows, leaving the top, and moving the cross up as far as possible. Gordon suggested just shooting the power point overheads onto a blank white wall then; we really wouldn't need screens. I say if we are going to have screens, they *need to be ones that can be pulled up and let down. The bigger question that needs answering though is, "are we going to change our current building to meet our needs for the next twenty years or do we still have a plan to expand within the next 10 – 15 years?"*

I suggest we all pray collectively and diligently together about this this summer before we move ahead with making structural changes to the building.

Thanks for listening

∞∞∞∞

Gordon is beginning his third year as part of the elder team, so we are both now part of the leadership team. The Child Protection Policy that has been a project of the elders for several years is finally passed. Background checks for nursery and youth workers is now instituted. Installation of windows in all the classroom doors and the kitchen was completed last year.

"Bible-saturated, Worship-based" prayer is introduced to the elders and other men who lead Sunday prayer as the Biblical and best way to pray. Instead of praying spontaneously, a passage of scripture is chosen and used as the prayer. "Worship-based prayer is God-centered, Scripture-driven, Spirit-led model for prayer born out of a pattern we see in Scripture to promote the fear of God, the will of God, and the all-consuming love for God to the glory of God," states a communication sent out by Pastor Travis to a select group of men. As part of the elder team, Gordon tries to follow the new guidelines. He has always been one to try to conform. He says, "yes," as often as possible when asked to pray but it has become a challenge and begins to feel very restrictive to try to pray with a strict set of guidelines. Other men simply decline when asked to pray.

Pastor Travis also begins to promote the training of men who will eventually be candidates for elders. He invites a chosen group of men to work through a comprehensive leadership training and teaching program published by (CCBT – Center for Church Based Training). The goal of this Bible Study is to "explore the essence of church leadership and develop life-changing convictions about what it means to be a spiritual servant leader conformed to the image of Christ."[12] The concepts of "servant leadership" and "shepherding" are introduced. The final goal is that these men will be prepared to serve as elders and it soon becomes evident that only these men will be included in the consideration for elders the following year.

∞∞∞∞

Gordon's Vacation Bible School project for the 2010 summer is building a swinging bridge between two (fake) trees in the church for use by the children in crossing the river (fake blue water) through the jungle. My brother and his family seem to have a habit of visiting when Gordon is in the throes of testing out his creations. This year, my brother declined to test it out and instead, Erin was elected to be the test subject. I was over by the house when I heard a scream from my brother's wife. The one "tree" holding the bridge didn't have strong enough "roots" and Erin almost took a dip in the "river." By the time VBS started, the trees and the bridge were ready for the safe passage of sixty children over and over.

Our daughter, Erin, is going to be a junior in high school this fall. She helps with AWANA as a leader after school on

Wednesday evenings. In July, she goes along with the youth group lead by Pastor Jack to St. Louis, MO. There they volunteer in fixing the homes of people who are too poor to do it themselves. While Pastor Jack is on the mission trip and Pastor Travis is on vacation, Gordon again preaches for the congregation. His sermon title is "Do you have reservations or a reservation?"

∞∞∞∞

March 4-5, 2011 finds key leaders and core families from the church gathering together at a local camp for a working retreat with the Evangelical Free Church district superintendent. The purpose of this meeting is to begin the "process of pursuing God's heart for the vision of the church." This grew out of "our desire to be a healthy church that intentionally pursues God's purposes."[13] The elders will take what has been brainstormed during this retreat and develop a new mission and vision statement for church. Gordon, as an elder, announces this coming statement to the congregation at the end of yet another of his sermons in December. "The elders and Pastor Travis have been working on an updated vision statement for our church. This is what we have come up with:

Our desire is to be a people who are loving Jesus, living the word, and serving people.
Again, that is, loving Jesus, living the word, serving people.
We want to be a people who love the light, not the darkness. Learning from the Word, the Bible, and applying it to our lives will cause us to add power to our light bulbs. TEFC will begin to shine for Christ in the community as each light shines brighter.

And we want to shine on people by serving them because we know that Jesus said, "I did not come to serve but to be served."

The mission statement presented and approved by the congregation at the annual meeting January 28, 2012 is

We exist to glorify God by loving Him with all our heart, delighting in His Word, and declaring His Gospel in the power of the Holy Spirit for the transformation of lives in a vital and joyful union with Jesus Christ.

Pastor Travis's conclusion is that "fulfilling this mission would mean TEFC is a *God-glorifying, love-motivated, Bible-saturated, gospel-driven, Spirit-empowered, transformational, Christ-centered* church." The intent of the new vision and mission statement, though a little lofty, sounds honorable and delightful. In looking back, though, I believe it opens the door to what will become an attitude of exclusivity and superiority at this church. It is what Larry Osborne calls the development of "accidental Phariseeism." In a desire to honor and pursue God, one ends up "unwittingly pursuing an overzealous model of faith that sabotages the work of the Lord we think we're serving... We have coined a host of buzzwords to let everyone know that our tribe is far more biblical, committed, and pleasing to the Lord than the deluded masses who fail to match up."[14]

2011 is a time of church growth in numbers. Pastor Jack spearheads many different outreaches. The third annual block party to the trailer park, the third annual Thanksgiving grocery give-away, and treat outreaches to the school district and the city of Corinth are held. And there are Friday night fires in the summer to enjoy each other's company. Much laughter is heard at them. Our daughter, Erin, is baptized in the Mississippi along with others in August during a joint service with our church plant in Ephesus. Lastly, Christmas brings the sponsoring of three needy families through the Giving Tree Project.

2011 is Gordon's last year of his elder term and he is growing weary of the high expectations from the pastor and is ready for a break. At the last elder meeting in December, a list is made of the vision for the future. Pastor Travis wants to start broadcasting the sermons, "Living the Word" recordings, to the community. He is eager to start the neighborhood outreaches proposed by the Outreach team, and he wants to begin sermon-based small groups. There is talk of going to multiple services in the next year due to the need for more people space until an addition can be built. And a facility building team is discussed with Gordon being suggested as the possible Chairman of this committee. Pastor Travis presents all the elders and administrative council members with an article on the "biblical" pathway to financing a building. To him this means, we are to have faith that God will supply the funds to build this debt free. There is no vote. He simply declares that this is how we are going to build. Gordon suggests that maybe we should plan and build cost effectively borrowing the money from the EFCA program, Christian Investors, like we did when first building the church. Lastly, Pastor Travis asks for an 8-week sabbatical in 2012. Gordon is the only one opposed but does eventually vote to allow it.

Chapter 10 Complementarianism -A Redefined Approach

For me personally, 2011 starts a chain of events on the Administrative Council that will initiate a crack in my commitment and allegiance to this church. A gentleman, whom I shall call Peter, is asked to join the AC. Peter is a fairly new comer to the church. He was baptized at Truth in 2006 and completed the class on men's leadership in 2010. He is seen as a good addition to the Administrative Council. He is motivated to get things accomplished. And he agrees to serve as the Financial Secretary for the church. This position falls under the oversight of the treasurer, the position in which I serve. His job is to record the offering donations and to send out tax statements at the end of the year. All seems to go well at first. Then early in the summer, one of the carpenters in the church, whom I shall call Moses, is asked to do some carpentry work around the church.

I arrive at the AC meeting as is my usual custom. After the usual pleasant chit-chat, we get started. Moses is a guest at our meeting. I am invited to give the financial report and then Peter addresses me, "I asked Moses to come tonight, so you could write a check for his work."

I am taken aback. No one has talked to me about this beforehand. "I don't have enough money in the checkbook to pay him tonight," I respond. "I need to transfer some money from savings first."

"I told Moses we would pay him tonight," Peter insists, "If you are not going to write him a check tonight, I will write him a personal check."

I am embarrassed and confused. I have not been included in any conversation informing me that I needed to have the money to pay Moses tonight. And now I am being put on the spot and made to look like I am incompetent and uncooperative. *What just happened here?*

A few weeks later, there is an e-mail conversation with the pastors about insurance on the building, what is to be paid, and for what but I am not included. I am upset and offended. I am the one who would have the answers to these questions. This has happened a couple of times now where Peter will address financial concerns with the pastors and other male AC members but will leave me, as the treasurer, out of the communication loop.

Then, without an explanation, he resigns from the Financial Secretary role. When I ask for the Quicken software back that we are using on our home computers, he is rude and condescending.

I write him an e-mail at the end of 2011 to which he does not respond.

I really want to embrace you as a brother in the Lord. I know that you work hard for the Lord and desire to do your best for the church. I, however, struggle continually with your practice of going around me to other people with information and questions about financial things. Why? I do not understand.

The information and questions about the insurance should be being directed to the AC – not the pastors. If only the pastors and the elders have decision making ability, they why do we have the AC? I find this continual behavior to be hurtful and demeaning. My desire is that we develop a collegial relationship where all such information is discussed and shared directly to all those who would benefit from the information. So my question is, what do you need from me in order to be able to feel like you can communicate with me? I don't feel that I can continue as treasurer if I do not have the trust and respect of those I need to work with on an ongoing basis. I have struggled over the last year trying to tell myself it doesn't matter but feeling disrespected translates into how I feel about all my interactions with the leadership in general. I cannot change that I am a woman and if this is the issue, then I feel I need to step down. Would you be willing to sit down with Pastor Travis and try to address this dynamic together? Thank you for considering this. Respectfully.

I sense that what has been happening is related to my being a woman though I have no proof of that. I am hurt and angered that he is allowed to treat me this way with what feels like no response from the elder board or pastors. At the beginning of 2012, Peter is asked to step into the Chairman of the Administrative Council role. During this short time of being chairman, he institutes a stricter following of Roberts Rules of Order and defers more of the final decisions on issues to the elders. There is discussion about outside groups use of the church facility and how this should be handled. He decides that the elders should review the Building Use Policy and update this policy. This he directs to them. Then in late summer, Peter chairs an AC meeting as usual. At the end, he tells us all, "I am resigning effective tonight." He gives no explanation or reason why but gets up and walks out. I sense that this has something to do with me.

It isn't until Pastor Travis eventually arranges a mediated meeting between Peter and I late in 2012, that I learn the truth. Peter resigned from his role as Financial Secretary because he did not believe a man should serve under a woman. And he showed his disagreement of women being in any leadership role by just going around me. Leaving the AC chairman role was his final protest against women being in leadership roles. Pastor Travis tells me several years later that they do try to counsel him that women are to be treated honorably and their input included in decisions. But from my perspective, I see no evidence of such. I am left feeling unsupported and discounted.

I approach Pastor Travis after the service one Sunday, "Ever since you have started pushing men's leadership, there seems to be a shift in the attitude of the leadership towards women." I share my frustration and irritation, "Women used to be able to contribute to decisions in the church. It seems that now only the men on the elder board can make decisions about the direction of the church."

His reaction is instantaneous. A twinge of anger creases his brow. He doesn't ask why I say that. He doesn't seek to explore my perspective.

"We are following what is Biblical," he shoots back. "The Bible instructs men to be the leaders. It's not true that we don't include women's opinions. I am a complementarian. Men and women have different but equal roles. And men are to be the leaders."

∞∞∞∞

So what does the term "complementarian" mean and where does it come from? The term "complementarian" was coined by The Council on Biblical Manhood and Womanhood (CBMW). "At a 1986 meeting of

75

the Evangelical Theological Society(ETS), Wayne Grudem gave a speech on 'Manhood and Womanhood in Biblical and Theological Perspectives' in which he invited delegates to join 'a new organization dedicated to upholding both equality and differences between men and women in marriage and the church.' This was followed by a meeting in Dallas with Grudem, John Piper, Wayne House, and others. A subsequent meeting was held in Danvers, Massachusetts; at this meeting, the Danvers Statement on Biblical Manhood and Womanhood was finalized.[15]

The Council on Biblical Manhood and Womanhood felt that they needed to come up with a new word besides "submission" and "patriarchy" which has negative connotations to most people, to describe someone who ascribes to the historic, "biblical" idea that male and female are equal but have different roles in society. It sounds really good when someone says they believe men and women are equal but are designed to complement each other, but it is a whole different story when one realizes that in real life, it means only the men are allowed to have the final vote regarding crucial decisions in the church or the home. Truth had always been a church in which only men held pastor and elder positions. This is the position that both Gordon and I came from in our past theological persuasions and had no problem with it, but I begin to see a difference in how this is carried out under the new "complementarian" label. It is one thing to consult and seriously consider the opinions of the women in the church before making decisions and another to begin to make decisions based only on the what the male leadership determines is the correct path. Of course, the leadership denies that they are not considering others thoughts, but I have begun to feel the tentacles of this change in leadership emphasis mostly in the form of dismissiveness over concerns that are expressed by me and other women and a leaning towards making decisions without consulting the congregation as a whole.

Danvers Statement on Biblical Manhood and Womanhood

Based on our understanding of Biblical teachings, we affirm the following:

Both Adam and Eve were created in God's image, equal before God as persons and distinct in their manhood and womanhood (Gen 1:26-27, 2:18).

Distinctions in masculine and feminine roles are ordained by God as part of the created order, and should find an echo in every human heart (Gen 2:18, 21-24; 1 Cor 11:7-9; 1 Tim 2:12-14).

Adam's headship in marriage was established by God before the Fall, and was not a result of sin (Gen 2:16-18, 21-24, 3:1-13; 1 Cor 11:7-9).

The Fall introduced distortions into the relationships between men and women (Gen 3:1-7, 12, 16).

In the home, the husband's loving, humble headship tends to be replaced by domination or passivity; the wife's intelligent, willing submission tends to be replaced by usurpation or servility.

In the church, sin inclines men toward a worldly love of power or an abdication of spiritual responsibility, and inclines women to resist limitations on their roles or to neglect the use of their gifts in appropriate ministries.

The Old Testament, as well as the New Testament, manifests the equally high value and dignity which God attached to the roles of both men and women (Gen 1:26-27, 2:18; Gal 3:28). Both Old and New Testaments also affirm the principle of male headship in the family and in the covenant community (Gen 2:18; Eph 5:21-33; Col 3:18-19; 1 Tim 2:11-15).

Redemption in Christ aims at removing the distortions introduced by the curse.

In the family, husbands should forsake harsh or selfish leadership and grow in love and care for their wives; wives should forsake resistance to their husbands' authority and grow in willing, joyful submission to their husbands' leadership (Eph 5:21-33; Col 3:18-19; Tit 2:3-5; 1 Pet 3:1-7).

In the church, redemption in Christ gives men and women an equal share in the blessings of salvation; nevertheless, some governing and teaching roles within the church are restricted to men (Gal 3:28; 1 Cor 11:2-16; 1 Tim 2:11-15).

In all of life Christ is the supreme authority and guide for men and women, so that no earthly submission-domestic, religious, or civil-ever implies a mandate to follow a human authority into sin (Dan 3:10-18; Acts 4:19-20, 5:27-29; 1 Pet 3:1-2).

In both men and women a heartfelt sense of call to ministry should never be used to set aside Biblical criteria for particular ministries (1 Tim 2:11-15, 3:1-13; Tit 1:5-9). Rather, Biblical teaching should remain the authority for testing our subjective discernment of God's will.

With half the world's population outside the reach of indigenous evangelism; with countless other lost people in those societies that have heard the gospel; with the stresses and miseries of sickness, malnutrition, homelessness, illiteracy, ignorance, aging, addiction, crime, incarceration, neuroses, and loneliness, no man or woman who feels a passion from God to make His grace known in word and deed need ever live without a fulfilling ministry for the glory of Christ and the good of this fallen world (1 Cor 12:7-21).

Amanda Farmer

We are convinced that a denial or neglect of these principles will lead to increasingly destructive consequences in our families, our churches, and the culture at large.[16]

Chapter 11 The Increase of Authoritarianism

There is much discussion amongst the Administrative Council and the Elder Board as to how to best prepare the front of the church so that we can record the sermons for public broadcasting. The elder present at our February AC meeting in 2010 reports to us, "We are going to do whatever it takes to make a top-notch product. If some people get their feelings hurt, they will have to deal with it."

I am taken aback by this attitude. This is a congregational style decision-making church (or at least, it used to be) and I am concerned. I approach the pastor, "I really want to encourage you as leaders to tread carefully in this regard. Is having a perfect product the ultimate goal? Is not the goal to reach more people for Christ? If in the process, one disregards the relationships already established and the wishes of the majority of the people, has Christ been honored? That membership is not being consulted in a decision that may result in major alterations of the building is of concern to me. Churches have split over far less and I don't want to see a rift develop here."

"We have not been proceeding without consideration as to how sensitive this issue can be for many at TEFC," he responds after thanking me for sharing my concerns. "Perfection and performance are certainly not our goal. However, we will not put out a poor-quality product because our mission of reaching people with the gospel will be defeated otherwise. We live in a culture where people are extremely screen-oriented and if the lighting and sound is poor, they will click to the next channel within seconds. We can't expect any one to 'tolerate' poor quality to hear our message. This decision cannot actually be a church-wide decision... The more people we involve, the more difficult the process will be. Let me assure you that I will do my best to lead our team in making a decision that best serves the mission of the gospel including making it in a way that is considerate of people."

Although I appreciate the thoughtful response of the pastor, I am bothered by the change in attitude that I see amongst the leadership in their approach to ministry. There is a leaning towards a more authoritarian style of leadership in which perfection has crept into the top priority position above relationships. Though it is subtle, it troubles me. "I am behind the elders and the pastors all the way in our new venture of trying to reach the community through TV broadcasting. I just want this to be a venture of TEFC that we are all behind – not just an elder and pastor venture."

Recognizing his response as a little hard-nosed, he sends me a note a few days later, "Amanda, I just want to make sure that I didn't bruise you in any way. If I did, I apologize. It was certainly not my intent. Just want to make sure. As I looked back at my communication again, I realized it might have come across kind of heavy. Just know that my heart toward you is good."

∞∞∞∞

I find adult Sunday School in 2012 to be enjoyable. During the spring, we go through the "Peacemaker" video series by Ken Sande. In *The Peacemaker*, Ken Sande presents a comprehensive and practical theology for conflict resolution designed to bring about not only a cease-fire but also unity and harmony. Sande takes readers beyond resolving conflicts to true, life-changing reconciliation with family members, coworkers, and fellow believers. In the fall, we start a study by Paul David Tripp using his book, *Instruments in the Redeemer's Hands.* Paul Tripp provides insights which I expect to find useful as a Gospel counsellor, but also in my walk as a maturing Christian seeking resources that will help me grow and understand Christ better. Tripp illuminates a dimension of the Word as wise counsel for people who are hurting and for people who would help them. He provides tools so that all believers can act as counsellors, using language that is easy to understand, offering illustrations that are easy to relate to.

I love leaning about how people function and respond. Craziness and dysfunction have always been a part of my family of origin, so I am invested in trying to understand what is happening in the minds of others. I also enjoy learning about techniques and principles for helping those who are struggling. This last study leads into the Pastoral team beginning Biblical Counseling training with Faith Biblical Counseling. Pastor Travis talks about eventually choosing and training a team of lay people to help in Biblical Counseling. I am interested in eventually participating in this.

∞∞∞∞

The Building Exploration Team is hard at work in 2012. The task of the seven-member team is to research church design and lay out a seven-phase building expansion plan that can be pursued in steps. The final goal is to build this proposed $2.2 million-dollar building debt-free. Gordon chairs this committee and spends many hours incorporating ideas into a preliminary plan. One of the members on this team is a man I shall call Vance. Vance has not been at the church for very many years, but Vance has significant talents. He has a background in road design and works in a supervisory capacity for the state. Vance has an assertive personality and has the tools to create sophisticated drawings. Gordon, even though he is the chairman, allows Vance to lead many of the meetings. Vance has many specific ideas on how to move this process forward. "I can't compete with him," Gordon shares with me one evening.

Vance comes to the building team meeting one evening and announces, "I have found a steel building that has been sitting around for a few years that we can buy for a discounted price of $50,000. I think this is the Lord telling us that this is the way to go."

As a result of this declaration, the previous plans and calculations are abandoned in favor of pursuing a plan that incorporates this large steel building. One day, Pastor Travis addresses Gordon, "Do you care if I put Vance in as the Chairman of the Building Committee?"

Gordon is hurt but what is he going to say? It sounds self-centered and unchristian to refuse. "No, go ahead." Gordon comes home demoralized and feeling like he has been dumped, but he tries to rationalize it away. *Vance's way better than I am, and he has already taken over, so he might just as well be chairman.*

∞∞∞

The Building Use Policy that has been sent to the elders has been a low priority item for them. Several months pass and nothing has been addressed on it. I offer to do the initial work on a new Building Use Policy, incorporating the ideas that we have discussed and typing up a first draft for the elders to work from.

The church office will review the request for the use of the building by a member and inform the applicant of its approval or disapproval. (A member is defined as an official member of TEFC and his immediate family – spouse, parents, children) All requests for use by non-members or organizations not affiliated with Truth Evangelical Free Church require approval by a Pastor or the Administrative Council.

Once approved, scheduling shall be done through the Church secretary. In most situations, official church functions will receive first priority for usage.

*If the application by a <u>non-member or organization not affiliated with TEFC</u> is approved, it will be scheduled once the deposit is received.

*Usage Fee for groups who are non-profit but secular in nature and for whom the use of the building is being allowed as an outreach to the community (ie Boy Scouts, cross country spaghetti supper) $50 per month or $25 per use if a one-time use

*Deposit and Usage Fees may be contracted at a different rate for longer term use, waived, or reduced by a majority vote of the Administrative Council

Usage Fee for non-profit groups whose main purpose is the furtherance of the gospel: $10 non-refundable fee per use
Usage Fee for groups who are for profit and/or for whom the whole building would be utilized (ie weddings, seminars)
$100 deposit (To be returned if the building and grounds are left in the same condition as found.)
$200 Non-refundable Fee for the use of the building and facilities

The major themes are that members will continue to be able to use the building free of charge as they always have while non-members will need to pay. The thought is that members most likely already contribute on a regular basis to the work and care of the church. Then it is simply a matter of deciding what is appropriate to charge to non-members and outside groups who wish to use the building. We are all in agreement that there should be a difference based on the mission and purpose of the group and how it coincides with the vision and purpose of the church. Groups that simply want to use the building for secular purposes would be treated differently (in payment required) than those who are committed to mutual furtherance of the gospel as their primary purpose. I type up the proposed policy and we send it on to the elders and pastors for discussion and changes/approval.

∞∞∞∞

September is the time at the church to address budget issues and as we come closer to that time, I realize that I am irritated and annoyed with the whole budget process. I am totally frustrated with the discrepancy between what the leadership says the budget means and how I am actually allowed to practice. I have put hours into a document that no one even thinks about the rest of the year when spending money. The elders change things at their discretion. People spend without me being able to deny them that privilege even if the funds are low. As the treasurer, I feel that once the budget is complete that I should be able to have the authority to regulate how the money is spent based on the budget and to be consulted before the elders make changes in how the cash flow is handled. This is what Samuel, the former banker-treasurer, was allowed to do. Now he is an elder and it seems like this, I believe to be unconscious, special treatment based on his gender and position in society has shifted to the elder board. Irritation rises up at the bias I sense. I firmly believe that the job description and role of the treasurer should not be shifting based on who is in that role. There are other feelings that mingle in me as I struggle with the shifts in principles I see creeping in. One has to do with the fact that I am a woman and the other has to do with a subtle increase in authoritarianism in the leadership.

"This has become a top-down organization with little input from the congregation," I express my frustration to the Pastor, "When one of the elders was asked at the AC meeting if they had considered the budget when deciding to spend increased amounts on outreach yet this year, his response was that 'the Lord told us to do it and we were moving ahead in faith no matter what the cost.'"

"This indicates to me that the leaders are leading like they should be," Pastor Travis replies.

I suck in my breath and let it out slowly. This whole attitude rankles me.

I just want to say that leading to me is more than just making decisions and then trying to get the people to follow. Maybe I can communicate my thoughts with an illustration.

As a married person in a Christian home, the husband is a leader in the home and the wife is his help meet. For illustration purposes, let's say that the husband and wife (who are both Christians) have agreed to not spend more than $500 personally without discussing the transaction together and agreeing to move forward together. This would be the same as the AC and elders agreeing with the congregation on a budget for the following year. It is essentially an agreement in which the congregation agrees at the annual meeting to supply the money to finance the church budget while the church agrees to stay within the guidelines of spending as set forth in the budget for that year. Let's just say then that the husband, as he becomes closer to Christ, is convicted that he should give $1000 in Bibles to China. He does so without discussing this with his wife. He just tells her that he has done it and thinks she should be excited about his new approach. He can't understand why she is so upset when all he was trying to do was honor the Lord. What if he says to her, "The Lord told me to do this and I'm going to do what I need to do to follow him regardless?" What is wrong in this leadership? Answer: He has not honored his wife. He has not communicated with her and they have not decided together.

I joined this church because it valued the input of the congregation. As the treasurer, especially, and on the administrative council, I feel my input should be sought. I think my biggest frustration is the lack of communication with me. It feels like disrespect to me for the position of treasurer and the person in it.

Soon after this communication, I get an e-mail from the pastor asking me to draw up a job description and to delineate my expectations of the treasurer role. "I hope and trust that this will reduce some of your frustration you have been experiencing over differing expectations that you, the elder board, and the pastors may have had."

It doesn't take me long to present the elders with the job description and the role of the treasurer as I see it.

Oversee and account for disbursement of all funds within budget guidelines. Be directly accountable to designated Financial Liaison on Elder Board. Balance the checkbook and provide financial reports on a monthly basis to AC, Elders, and pastors. No decision on how funds will be collected and dispersed will be made without treasurer consultation. If a question arises as to funds disbursement above what is budgeted in Elder Board categories, Elders would make the final decision with input from the treasurer as to the state of the checkbook and expected expenses.

If a question arises as to funds disbursement above what is budgeted in AC Board categories, the AC would make the final decision with input from the treasurer as to the state of the checkbook and expected expenses.

Treasurer would have input into pastors and administrative assistant salaries.

I am soon summoned to a meeting with two elders for the purpose of informing me that the treasurer will not be making any decisions in that role. Even though he is at church on this day, the banker-elder and former treasurer refrains from attending.

∞∞∞∞

The Outreach Team begins Neighborhood Outreaches in the fall 2012. A section of the city is chosen for each outreach. Bags are filled with tracts and goodies to deliver to each home in that area. Prayer and friendship are offered to all who answer their door. We feel overwhelmed by all the activity expectations in this approximately 130 people congregation and do not participate in the Neighborhood Outreaches. I notice that very few other people participate either outside of the outreach committee members' and pastor's families.

We do, however, agree to host one of the small sermon-based groups that is launched in the fall. We enjoy having people at our home and the fellowship it provides. The other plans for the church in 2012, starting TV broadcasting of the service and going to two worship services never do get off the ground. The number of people attending has dropped back down and the plan for two services is abandoned. The broadcasting plan is never launched for unknown reasons. "We are waiting for the computer tech man to get things set up," does not seem like a valid reason after the waiting goes on for ten years.

Chapter 12 A New Dynamic Is Added To the Leadership

Gordon continues to be active on the building committee and it is around this time that rumor starts to circulate that Kwik Trip, a popular gas station/convenience store chain, is looking to buy land upon which the city compost site now sits. This is exciting news for the church as the compost pile is a sore spot for the church. We must drive through the compost site every time that we come to church as it is our only access. When the church was built in 1989, an easement was granted through city property with the hope that at some later date, a permanent access could be obtained. Now there is hope that this might be possible. As the year progresses, Kwik Trip has started to negotiate with the city for this property and if they are able to buy it, they will build and pay for an access to the church and their property in exchange for a small portion of church land. In addition, they will give the church $100,000 as a good faith gift. This development seems to be the leading of the Lord for finalizing something that has long been prayed for and for kickstarting the building project.

Gordon also continues to attend the men's leadership group throughout the year. A gentleman from the Fidelis Foundation, Joe Smith, is brought in to lead the group. In December, Gordon is asked again if he will run for an elder position. Feeling that in many ways he cannot support some of the changes in the direction of the church and still weary from the heavy expectation of being an elder, he declines.

∞∞∞∞

The first week in June 2013, we host a graduation/going away party for Sonya, our foreign exchange student from Russia. She has spent nine months with us. For me, it was a challenging nine months. I had stipulated on the application that I did not want a student who found Christianity offensive. Her first weekend in our home, we attend a baptism in the Mississippi River. As we are driving home, in her limited English, she announces that she does not want to go to church again. Well, that's a problem as that is what we do every Sunday. How did this happen? I sob on the phone to the area representative. This is exactly what I did not want to happen when I agreed to sign up for this. She offers to move her but not wanting to renege on my commitment, I plow onward. I finally make what I think is a reasonable deal with Sonya. She will work in the nursery while we attend church and my only other requirement is that she attend youth group on Sunday evenings with Erin who is in her first year at the community college. In spite of this compromise, we struggle continually with a reluctance on her part to participate in anything having to do with our faith. It puts a constant tension in our lives that I never learn to deal with constructively.

We do have many enjoyable experiences and times together and I love our talks as a family in the evenings. At the end of the year, I plan a graduation and going away party. I invite school friends and our church family. After what seems to be a fun and enjoyable evening, Sonja opens all of her gifts and takes them to her room except for those from the church people. They sit in a chair untouched. I sense that there is a problem. I pick up a few of the cards and read them. Many have Christian affirmations and Bible verses. Later she comes upstairs. "I want you to return all those gifts and cards to the church people," she demands, "you made me go to the youth group when I didn't want to."

"No, I am not going to give them back." I refuse to return gifts given with kindness. "I would expect when you come here as a foreign exchange student that you would be somewhat open to experiencing the culture of your host family."

"I am going to live with the neighbor for the rest of the week until it is time to go home," she fires back.

I am distressed at the ending of this experience. I am definitely not cut out to be a mother to a teenager from a different culture who comes with very specific expectations and set beliefs. And I don't think I will ever be doing this again.

∞∞∞∞

Adult Sunday School in 2013 is taught using two books, *The Gospel-Centered Life* and *The Gospel-Centered Community* by Robert Thune and Will Walker. Each of these studies has useful principles on which to meditate and to help us grow in our walk with Christ and each other. I especially enjoy the Gospel-Centered community study. I think we are just studying concepts that hopefully we will incorporate in our lives in living with others in the church. I do not realize until later that this study may have purposefully been chosen with the intent of leading this church towards an actual written covenant structure in the future. One of the chapters is on "An Honest Community." It stresses that "authentic community means being known 'as we really are.' But most of us are worried that others would not accept us or like us if they really knew us."[17] I particularly remember a question that is asked in class one Sunday, "What would happen if we all were transparent and let others see exactly who we are instead of wearing masks?"

My dear husband under his breath responds, "I would have to find another church."

I do not realize how prophetic this is to become. The class also spends much time emphasizing how in caring for each other and knowing each other that we will pursue those who are struggling, that the community will not just let people walk away from the church.

∞∞∞∞

2013 sees a change in four of the seven Administrative Council member positions. Since the resignation of Peter, a gentleman named Charles has been appointed to the chairman role. Charles is a dedicated Christian. He is a servant-leader and is open to the input of those under him but not very assertive. Additionally, a husband and wife separately are asked to serve on the AC and they both say yes. Lastly, Vance who is now leading the Building Exploration Committee is asked to join. Vance is seen as a go-getter and someone who will be a huge asset in driving forward the tasks of the AC. He agrees to accept the position of secretary on the council.

One of the items on the July meeting agenda is the Building Use Policy. After two years, it has come back to us from the Elders with a request to make some changes. The elders feel the usage fee schedule is too complex and has "too many dollar signs." But they do not specify which items exactly they feel need changing nor do they offer any guidance or suggestions as to what they would like to see. They seem to have forgotten that more than half of the AC has changed since this revamping of the policy began and these members are not aware of what previous work and discussions have occurred. The elder sitting in on the meeting does not attempt to clarify what is expected either.

Vance begins to read through the policy and starts to lobby for changing each point one by one. Traditionally, it has always been understood that members will be allowed to use the building for free. Now, that is thrown out under Vance's push to have everyone pay for the use of the building. When one member brings up the point that not everyone can pay, it is suggested that a clause be included that "Pastors can, at their discretion, waive these fees." I am becoming increasingly frustrated and upset as the meeting progresses. My stomach ties into a knot. So what is the point of having guidelines if we nullify them by allowing the pastors to override any policy finalized? That should be the function of the Administrative Council.

The meeting continues with suggestions being made and then a vote being called for over and over. What has happened to our respect for one another I wonder? Vance continues to lobby for his positions and others follow his lead. There is no gatekeeper in this group and no real leader to bring us back to what we have always considered as an important dynamic – being sensitive to each other and trying to reach a consensus or at least an outcome that all can live with. It is like the positions of I and another long-time member of the group are being railroaded over.

No one even seems to notice. I begin to feel nauseated and I begin to shake. I finally get up and walk out. The tears run down my cheeks as I drive home. What kind of a group do I belong to? The dynamics of this meeting have taken me back to the feelings of the overbearing insensitive ways of my father. I am so upset that I cannot sleep, I cannot eat, and I cannot think to function at work for several days. I cannot do this anymore.

After a long discussion with Pastor Travis, I inform him that I am resigning from the treasurer role.

"Will you continue to do the treasurer duties while we look for a new treasurer?" he asks.

"Yes," I respond. I love taking care of the financial end of things. The only thing that will be different is that I will not be attending leadership meetings. Maybe this is best anyway, I conclude, as it removes any conflict of interest if Gordon should be asked to run for elder again.

∞∞∞∞

In August, the elder team, Vance, and Joe Smith hold a private daylong retreat devoted to prayerfully processing the initial direction for expansion of the church facility. A *Building on the Cornerstone* brochure is developed at this meeting for distribution to the congregation. It outlines the seven steps of how the leadership wishes to proceed in this building venture. The Building Exploration Team has been dissolved and a Building Relay Team has been appointed. The Building Relay Team will consist of Pastor Travis, Vance, and two others with the purpose of collecting data and input from the congregation and working alongside the architect in developing a concrete plan. I am annoyed that the pastor and Vance make up half of the Building Relay Team. In Gordon and my opinion, this is not a committee the pastor should be on. He himself admits that he knows nothing about building and his job is to lead the church spiritually. I wonder if this is an indication of a subtle need to be in control of what is happening with "his" church? He also seems to have become enamored with the characteristics that Vance displays. Vance is used to being a leader of a secular company and his idea of leadership is to make the decisions and then vehemently sway others toward his opinion. This approach, Travis seems to be drawn to. I am dismayed that Travis is blind to what is subtly happening to him.

Chapter 13 Betrayal & Rejection

Gordon begins to again think about whether he should accept a spot on the elder board if asked. We both believe he will be asked. There is no reason that they would not ask. He said no last year just because he needed some more time away to regroup. Gordon struggles with this decision. We pray about it and he wrestles with whether he is prepared spiritually and mentally to meet the challenges and expectations Pastor Travis has for his elders. He finally makes the decision that he will say yes when asked. December comes and goes but no one asks. No candidate is published for consideration. Finally, at the annual meeting in January 2013, it is announced to the congregation, "No one could be found willing to step into the elder role." Therefore, they will run with only three elders and not four. Shock and disbelief flood through us. NO ONE could be found?? How can they say that? No one asked Gordon. What does that mean for my loyal dedicated husband. He finally gets up the courage to ask a remaining elder, "Why wasn't I considered for the elder position?"

"You didn't have enough faith," was the shocking answer.

What??? What is that supposed to mean? Gordon's competency first and now his faith has been called into question in the last two years. Gordon is deeply hurt, and we pull back from our involvement in the church. It is the beginning of a slide from which he will not recover. "I was good enough to hold the church together when there was no pastor but now I am suddenly not good enough?" So, what is happening that the church is not able to find men to fill the role of elder? One man's take on the matter is "all we learned by going to men's leadership group was that none of us are good enough to be elders." That is one aspect but there is the other aspect of the leadership becoming very exclusive as to who will be asked.

∞∞∞∞

As 2014 rolls around, I have been unofficially handling the finances of the church for five months while I wait for them to find a new treasurer. I have tried diligently to work with the elders, pastors, and administrative council members in a less sensitive and reactive manner and to be more approachable. I feel I have grown emotionally and in understanding of myself and that I am ready to return to the treasurers' role. Also, one of my thought processes was that I was expecting that Gordon would be asked to serve as an elder again in 2014 and I thought it better if I stepped aside in order to not cause any unnecessary conflict of interest. However, Gordon has not been asked to serve again as an elder, so it seems appropriate to me, since the treasurer role has not been filled, to seek to step back into the treasurer position. After all, I was the one who made the decision to step down. It was not a result of misconduct or disciplinary action.

In my naivety, I send an e-mail to Pastor Travis letting him know of my decision.

"I would like to step back into the treasurer role since I am performing all the duties of said role anyway except attending the AC meetings. If this is not a possibility, this is my notice that I will cease to perform these duties and will turn the computer in to the elders at the end of February." In my mind, I am simply telling them that I am giving them two months to find someone if they do not wish for me to be treasurer. I am feeling like they are not truly putting any effort into finding a replacement as long as I complete these significant duties for them. It is time to give them a deadline.

"We need to get together to talk about this as soon as possible," shoots back Pastor Travis.

I sense a cool tone in his message and my stomach muscles tighten. I feel like I am being summoned to the principal's office. With much trepidation, I enter his office a few days later. My sixth sense has not betrayed me. Pastor Travis is resolute, "You will not be stepping back into the treasurer role. The way you went about this was manipulative and we are not going to be manipulated."

I am caught off guard. Manipulative?? I feel like I have been slapped. This is a label that applies to my family of origin and I am extremely hurt. I try to explain to him my thought process to no avail. I am not trying to manipulate anything. I just want them to actively work towards getting another treasurer. I don't think it is fair to me for them to continue to expect me to carry out these responsibilities while they are laissez faire about a replacement.

"You have a problem with relationships and dealing with others. I am your friend and I am concerned about you. You have told me about situations at work that you haven't handled well as well as with your family and you cannot be in a leadership position until these issues are taken care of."

"Well, then be a mentor to me and help me develop my responses when different issues come up in the treasurer role," I plead.

His face is set in a firm line. He has already made his decision. "No."

So, all the problems I have shared with the pastor over the years are being thrown back at me and used as ammunition against me. My head hanging in shame and with tears streaming down my face, I get up, spin around and walk out of his office. Now I am angry. I drive home, grab the church computer, drive to the bank, march to Samuel's office at the bank, and plop the computer on his desk. "There you are. It's yours now."

Chapter 14 Our Frustration Mounts

E arly in February, Vance updates the congregation on the Kwik Trip developments and the building expansion. Kwik Trip is in the process of negotiating the final design with the city. This is a complicated process as there has to be agreement between the church, Kwik Trip, the city, and the Department of Transportation. As for the agreement between Kwik Trip and the church, all those things the church has asked of them, they are willing to include in the contract. The hope was that Kwik Trip would be able to close on the land purchase in May, but the date has been moved back to February 15, 2015 by the city. This is a huge disappointment as everyone was excited about the prospect of an official access for the church property.

Vance also reports that he has interviewed two architects for a proposal on a site rendering or plan drawing. The Building Relay Team holds several informational meetings over the next couple of months. The pastor and Vance continue to advocate for the buying of the steel building and the architect is directed to draw up plans incorporating this idea. Gordon and I, along with numerous others, make it plain that we feel the church is getting the cart before the horse, so to speak. The original building committee never finished their study looking at the various options as that was abandoned once Vance found the discounted steel building. "It would have been better if we had never heard of a discounted steel building," is my husband's take on the matter. The Kwik Trip purchase and entrance necessary has not been finalized and we do not have enough land to actually build the building that is being proposed. We suggest that the $145,000 from Kwik Trip, once we get it, should go towards land purchase as a first priority. Second, we should not even be thinking about purchasing anything until we have at least $600,000 saved for several reasons. Luke 14: 28 says "For which one of you when he wants to build a tower, does not first sit down and calculate the cost to see if he has enough to complete it? Otherwise, when he has laid a foundation and is not able to finish it, all who observe it begin to ridicule him."

The architect said at the first meeting that if we buy the building and store it, it will need to be kept dry if it is not to deteriorate. If we erect the shell only (hay storage barn style) and then it sits there for five years while we raise enough funds to continue, is not the same thing going to happen? The building is exposed to the weather and deteriorating while we fund raise.

It seems that things are being driven by the push to buy this building now because if we don't, the good bargain might be gone. If the Lord really wants us to have it, it will still be available when we truly have the funds to begin construction. Yes, the Lord can provide but he also expects us to not run ahead of Him.

I think at this point we should be concentrating on fund raising only while we put the time and resources necessary this year into securing a new associate pastor and administrative assistant as a first priority. Give the Lord a chance to work. Spending $10,000 for an architect rending of a building that may not be the final product to me is a total waste of money. This church has commenced a church expansion three or four times over the span of its existence and never moved on to completion.

∞∞∞∞

As a result of the various changes in leadership style, the elevation of the complementarian position, and the growing frustrations with how our voice is being disregarded, I write an open letter to the elders and the pastor in late February.

We love Pastor Travis. He is a charismatic leader and people follow him. Gordon and I do not want to see him leave. Furthermore, we believe he is sincere in wanting to build a Godly church and has a genuine relationship with Christ. I know we all want to build a church that honors God, is spiritually healthy, and growing. We are not trying to cause division. However, I feel we need to address some issues that I have seen developing over the last few years if we are going to grow into a church who is able to reach others for Christ with the greatest effectiveness especially with the building project coming up and also the need for a new assistant pastor.

The leadership team has gradually changed from pursuing a collaborative congregational approach guided by an effort to reach consensus while soliciting the spiritual wisdom of other members of the leadership teams and the congregation to one of a more corporate structure in which the elders and the "CEO" make the decisions. I do not feel this is the style of leadership envisioned by those who founded the church nor is it what we want to see in the leadership of the church we attend. Additionally, it has not been a good thing that there have been only two functioning elders over the last year as it allows a very unhealthy situation in which the stronger person can potentially sway most decisions towards his perspective. Consciously or unconsciously, the attitude that the elders and pastor exclusively are receiving leading from the Holy Spirit and that input from the AC or other members of the congregation is not needed is being perceived. There is a definite projection of "we have the authority from God" and "our decisions can't possibly be the wrong ones."

I am in disbelief that the leadership would prevent someone from being a part of a leadership team simply because that someone expresses a different position on an issue or expresses an opposing opinion. For a church to be optimally effective, there needs to be different points of view present by those in leadership – not a culling of those who do not fit the mindset of those already in leadership. This is how churches who are scripturally way off base develop.

I believe this change in the leadership operational paradigm is a result of the heavy emphasis on men's leadership in the last few years. There is nothing wrong with training men to lead but it has swung too far to the opposite extreme. The men in leadership have come to believe that this is leading – to make the decisions and expect everyone to follow. What happened to "servant leadership?" "Servant leadership" is talked about all the time but it is not practiced. My view of servant leadership is totally different from this.

Maybe some of this perception is because there is virtually no communication from the leadership to the congregation on a week to week basis. It is believed that elder meeting discussions are confidential (which some of them should be) to the point that decisions are made regarding the direction of the church with the congregation being totally uninvolved until the announcement is made well down the road when the decision is already made.

Along with this has developed an exclusivity of who is allowed into leadership. It seems that if a man has not attended the leadership class that he is not eligible to be an elder. The strict interpretation of the criteria required to be an elder, I believe, has removed all but a select few from participating in leadership. In the process, many good men have been left out of any leadership role. They have been left to feel that they are not good enough. And the elder positions are not filled.

The other, possibly unintended, consequence of the overemphasis on men's leadership is that the women have been left totally out of any actual leadership roles. The only ministries open to women in the church now are kitchen duty, teaching children's Sunday School or Children's church, nursery, and baking and cooking for meals. We have become very polarized as to men and women's roles. Men no longer are assigned in the nursery or children's church, or the kitchen. No women count money (except me in the past), no women ever read scripture from the front, or facilitate an adult Sunday School lesson, or lead a Life Group.

The elders, pastors, and church as a whole are missing the crucial different and balancing perspective by excluding women from the important decisions regarding the direction of the church...

Gordon and Amanda Farmer

∞∞∞∞

As I begin to think about not being allowed to step back into the treasurer role, I realize that I sometimes come across as intimidating and that I struggle with expressing my thoughts too freely. I humbly write an apology to the leadership.

I humbly submit that my intent has never been to usurp the authority of the elders. I am sorry that I have not always been approachable and have not always responded in a gracious way when I felt dismissed and not included in discussions that pertained to the treasurer's position. I had over the last six months after resigning from the AC attempted to correct these attitudes and responses so that I would not be so threatening. I felt that I was being successful, and I felt I was prepared to try again to rejoin the AC.

Enter disastrous recent interaction with my request to rejoin the AC being denied. I am beseeching you to turn the clock back two months and start over here? I am asking for your forgiveness for my past failures and am requesting that I be allowed a chance to demonstrate my desire to work together again harmoniously for the remainder of this year until the end of January 2015. Samuel can then have the treasurer role back if he so desires or if he has found someone else, they can have it for a couple of years. I promise to do the budget as desired by the elders regardless of my personal opinions. I understand that the same personalities exist on the AC and I may need help dealing with those dynamics.

Those who are currently members on the Administrative Council are asked if they have any objections to my returning to the treasurer role. There are no objections, so I am allowed to again step into the role of church treasurer.

Chapter 15 *The Leadership Makes the Decisions*

In late April, a joint meeting of the Elder Board and the Administrative Council is called to discuss the progress so far with the building project. A date of June 2 had previously been set for a members vote on two items. The first question will address if the congregation feels we should move ahead with preparations to expand our facility debt-free and the second question will address if we should move ahead with buying the reduced cost steel structure. Of course, all this depends on funds/donations being available. On this evening, Vance leads the meeting. There is a vigorous discussion. Many reservations are expressed about how fast we are moving with this project and it is suggested that we delay the congregational vote until negotiations with Kwik Trip become more concrete. Heads are nodding yes as most people agree with this approach.

Vance, however, wants this vote to proceed. "I told the seller I would let him know by the end of June if we are buying. We have to keep our word. I am not going to go back and tell him we haven't decided," he presses. "And besides, the Lord brought this building to our attention. How can you not see that this is His will?"

It is one of those guilt messages Christians like to use. After all, who wants to go against the Lord's will? When a vote is taken on whether to proceed with the June 2 vote, only I vote against doing so. The outcome of the congregational vote on June 2 is split but a majority do vote to proceed with the building as planned and to purchase the steel building.

"And by the way," adds Pastor Travis, "any donations towards the building fund, we are going to tithe 10% of that to missions."

"When did he decide that?" an elder board member directs his comment to me, "The elders never decided that."

In just a few months, this authoritarian decision will also cause a problem for me as treasurer. There are people who come to me and ask, "Can I just donate to the building fund? I don't want 10% of my money going somewhere else." Now I am stuck between a rock and a hard place. I believe it should be a person's choice where their money goes especially if they are already tithing 10% of their income to the general fund. I argue for a position of allowing these people that choice. I also point out that not allowing people the right to decide how their money is handled will result in people simply not giving.

"That's not going to happen," is the response, "This is an elder decision and not a treasurer one. We are going to honor God as a church by tithing. Just give us the names of those who are having a problem with this and we will talk to them."

Even if I remembered the names of all those with this request, I would not share them. I am frustrated with this selective decision making. As far as I know, there is no plan on how or where this 10% will be distributed.

∞∞∞∞

Pastor Jack, as the associate pastor, and Jill, as the administrative assistant for the pastors, have served faithfully at Truth for five years. In early 2014, Jack announces that he is leaving to move with his wife to Wisconsin. They have served tirelessly and faithfully during their time at the church, not only with the youth, but in many areas of outreach.

An Associate Pastor Search Team is appointed. This time neither Gordon nor I are asked to participate. Our expectations and desire for our church is far removed from what the pastor has set a course for. I am not surprised, though, when I see that one of the members of the search team is Pastor Travis himself. He is still on the Building Relay Team and now he is also on the search committee for a new pastor. This is what I call a desperate need for controlling the outcomes of whatever is happening. I point out to the Chairman of the Elder Board that this is a violation of the 2013 Constitution of the church, "Upon announcement that a search committee is being formed, any member may present a nomination to the Elder Board for their consideration. None of these nominees are to be members of the staff/office personnel."[18]

What I would expect from leaders with integrity, at that point, would be an admission of a mistake and a replacement of the pastor with a member at large. No, I am not opposed to the pastor having input into the candidate chosen to be his co-laborer, but I do think the influence from a powerful authoritarian personality on a search committee is far too great for there to be equal and impartial input by all. Instead the Elder Chairman contacts the North Central District office of the EFCA for advice. He then informs the congregation of what has happened and that the NCD told them it is "OK." Therefore, no changes will be made. "It is too late to make a change." *Is it ever too late to do the right thing?* I don't think so. But Pastor Travis validates my underlying suspicions with his response to my questions about this later. "I needed to be on the search committee to make sure that the candidate was compatible with me." He is afraid that he might have to serve with someone who does not share his vision for leadership and his particular Biblical interpretations.

∞∞∞

In July 2014 Pastor Travis's wife, Susan, is hired into the administrative assistant role to replace the departed Jill. Many of us think this is a really bad idea but the congregation is not consulted. Our concern is that there is too much power concentrated in the senior pastor's hands. But the elders, obviously, don't see it as a problem or alternatively, don't have the strength to squash this unwise decision.

Right about this time, it has come to the attention of Pastor Travis that Vance's stepson is planning on attending the EFCA divinity school in Deerfield, Illinois. Travis does some research and discovers that if the church has a scholarship fund for students attending the Trinity Evangelical Divinity School, that the school will match dollar for dollar for tuition up to a certain amount. Wanting to help this particular young man, he is excited about starting a scholarship fund. The elder board wastes no time in adopting a TEFC Christian Graduate School Match Policy for the express purpose of supplying funds to this young man to go to divinity school. The policy is to encourage *young men* to pursue a MDiv decree.

As the treasurer, I feel it is my duty to be responsible to see that tax laws are followed, and I have huge concerns about this proposal. I point out that this is borderline and against IRS policy. The overriding principle is that the contribution deduction requires the gift be "to or for the use of" a charitable entity, not an individual. To qualify, the gift must be to the church, knowing it will be used for scholarships, but without knowing who will receive the scholarship. A gift designated for a specific individual will not qualify. The scholarship must be open to all those who meet the criteria. The scholarship must be awarded on an objective and nondiscriminatory basis. The policy must contain the words "Scholarships are awarded without regard to sex, race, nationality, or national origin." Lastly, family members who choose to donate through this fund cannot take a tax deduction for their donation.

I try to impress on the pastor that the church is pushing the line with this scholarship. They are choosing to benefit one specific individual, they are discriminating by saying only young men can receive this scholarship, and the scholarship is not being rewarded on an objective basis. They have no intention of using it for other individuals. With all these issues present, I suggest that the best approach may be to simply give him a gift to help with his schooling. They do agree to drop the "young man" phrase from the policy but inform me that they intend to move ahead with their scholarship fund regardless of my objections. To me this is an unethical decision, but as has become the case over the last few years, my voice and advice are disregarded and dismissed. My respect for the leadership is slowly starting to erode and an anger is beginning to build at what I see as a disregard for choosing integrity over personal desire and a subtle disrespect for those who are offering them Godly wisdom.

Soon after this incident, my fear of too much power in the office comes to haunt me. Susan requests that the church procure a credit card that she and both pastors can use in purchasing items for the church. In the past, they have always used their personal credit cards and then turned in the receipts for reimbursement. This required them to keep track of the purchases and categorize them before being reimbursed. I liked this approach as it required accountability on their part. Having a church credit card opens the possibility of spending without being aware of how much is being spent and it also requires someone to keep track of what items are being spent and for which ministry. I can see myself spending numerous hours tracking down the receipts and trying to figure out which budget category to apply the purchase to. I can understand that they don't want these charges on their personal credit card though. "I will pursue getting a church credit card as long as you understand that keeping track of these purchases will be your responsibility," I impress my very firm position on this to Susan, "I am not going to spend hours sorting through purchases."

I think that we have an agreement. As I look into getting a card, it becomes evident that in order to apply for one, someone needs to put their personal social security number on the application in spite of the fact that it is for a non-profit corporation. I am reluctant to do this as Gordon and I have started to toss around the idea of leaving this church. I do not want to be responsible for the debts of a church I no longer even attend. But I can find no other way around it and I reluctantly apply for the card with my own social security number.

I find myself in a tight spot within the first month. I stop at the church to pick up the bills and realize that the credit card statement has not been sorted through or the amounts applied to any categories. "Oh, we got an e-mail from Samuel, an elder, stipulating that it will be your job to sort through the credit card statement," Susan explains. "I am following the elders' directions."

Now I am angry. "I explained to you my expectations before I got this card for you. It is none of the elders' business who sorts through the card. They have no business making this decision without talking to either you or me." This management from the top with no communication makes my blood boil. They would never have done this to him when Samuel was the treasurer. He would not have stood for it.

"Do whatever you want," I finally recognize that she is not going to go against an elder edict. I turn to walk out before I say something inappropriate.

"Wait, I will get Pastor Travis to help us work this out," Susan calls after me.

That should be a winner. The pastor is husband to the administrative assistant. Whose side is he going to favor? There is nothing unbiased here. We do not reach an agreement in this meeting and I resolve to just do what I need to do for right now. Not another word is spoken about this, but Susan does begin to sort through and categorize each bill.

Chapter 16 A New Pastor and Enter the New Calvinism

I n October, a new associate pastor arrives. Joshua is young, in his mid-20s, married, and the father of two young children. He has been attending classes at Southern Baptist Theological Seminary and plans to continue to earn his degree there on-line. He is smart and very adept at teaching and responding to challenges to his beliefs. What I know nothing about at the time is that Southern Baptist Theological Seminary is considered "ground zero" for the growing resurgence of Calvinism.[19]

∞∞∞∞

Being back on the Administrative Council goes well for six months until Vance is promoted to the position of AC Chairman in October 2014. He is replacing a gentleman that moved away in July. Everything changes overnight. Vance comes to the meetings with an agenda that has already been determined. He behaves as if he sees himself as the CEO of a company who makes the decisions and the purpose of the meeting is to communicate them to the next people in the chain of command. He has determined that we are changing the structure of the administration council and how it will function, the duties of each member, and how we conduct business. I spend a significant amount of time drawing up a diagram showing how I see the current organizational structure of the church. This is for the benefit of most of those who are on the AC who also have limited history with the church. He takes it from me and shoves it into the back of his notebook, never to even look at it.

Any discussion is timed and any attempt to reach a consensus has been abandoned. I am starting to have panic attacks at night again several days before the meeting and major anxiety for several days after the meeting. How should I handle this? Some of the newer ones in the group don't see a problem with this. Others do but don't want to openly challenge the leadership. By the end of the third meeting of his chairmanship, I can no longer remain silent.

"I am having a problem with how the meeting is being run and timed. It does not allow time for anyone to disagree or to actually discuss the merits of what is being proposed. It just feels like everything is already decided and that there is no hope for anyone's voice to be heard."

"You can't always have your way," is the snide remark directed my way. "I don't know why anyone would come to a meeting just to have conflict."

Ouch! "These kinds of comments do not provide a safe environment for expressing concerns," I quietly point out. Vance's guilt producing comments have had their effect. I shut up.

So I am back in the same situation with the same personality during which I resigned the last time. I don't know what to do. Sometimes, the Lord does work in unexpected ways. Within two months, a dramatic situation arises that causes Vance to follow his wife in leaving the church. This means that the AC chairman position is empty again. Thank you, Lord for intervening.

∞∞∞∞

As December rolls around again, Gordon and I discuss whether there is any chance that the elders will ask him again to be a candidate for elder. In some ways, he wants to serve again and in other ways, he no longer feels worthy or acceptable in the sight of the leadership. How does one regain the confidence to lead properly after one has been told that he "doesn't have enough faith?" Yes, this person who actually spoke the words apologized but that does not remove the words spoken or the damage done. The rest of the leadership who participated in this hurt have remained silent.

"They will just be asking because they feel like they have to since I made such a stink about it," is Gordon's perception of the situation. With all that is going on in the church, I encourage Gordon to consider accepting the role if he is asked. I make up my mind that if he is asked, I will resign as the treasurer to avoid any conflict of interest in having both of us in leadership roles. That was basically the plan anyway when I ask to be reinstated in 2014 and I am ready to step away from a role that seems to cause me more anxiety and conflict than I wish to deal with anymore.

Gordon and I sit in a small Sunday School room with both pastors and two of the elders. Butterflies flitter around in our stomachs. We have agreed to an interview with this group in response to Gordon being asked to consider accepting the elder role.

"What do you see as problems facing the church?" is one of the questions sent our way.

"We are concerned about the number of people coming in from other churches who seem to have a belief system different than ours. They seem to believe that everything is pre-determined by God and that we have no choice. Charles, one of these people who is now teaching Sunday School, even said that evil events such as 911 are God's will. That just is not true."

A long silence follows along with a few shrugs. No one addresses this statement but instead moves on to the next question.

"Do you think it is a good idea for both of you to be in leadership positions at the same time considering how contentious it can get at times?"

"We have served together in the past without a problem, so I think we could, but we have already talked about this," I respond. "I will resign from the treasurer's role and allow Gordon the opportunity to serve without needing to worry about me."

"But you are doing so much better. I have seen gradual improvements in your ability to interact with others and we really need you in the treasurer's role. Samuel will just be leaving the elder's role this year and I have not truly appreciated the toll it has taken on him. He really needs some time off to rest," Pastor Travis explains.

We leave the meeting somewhat confused. So why was Gordon even asked if they would rather have me than him? Are they saying both of us could be on at the same time? Gordon, however, has made up his mind. "They showed no interest in wanting me. It's like I said, they only asked because they felt like they had to." He declines to be on the ballot for elder.

At the annual meeting in January 2015, Charles is voted in as the next elder. A resolution is also passed to change the Constitution to allow for only three elders instead of four. I vote no. The pastors have started to refer to themselves as part of "the elder team," a move that I see as a subtle means of moving towards including themselves in the voting leadership, something the founders of the church purposely wanted to prevent from happening by including a prohibition to such in the Constitution.

Pastor Travis's annual report contains this declaration: *"We grow in our understanding and practice of being a gospel-centered, covenant-community which will strengthen the meaning of membership at TEFC. We also want to grow in leadership development. The first step in this direction will be for our current elders to develop a simple but intentional shepherding plan though which they can offer more intentional care to our members."*[20] This statement alone should have set off warning bells, but I don't see the warning signs until I look back at it later.

∞∞∞∞

Throughout the last Sunday School year, Charles, the newly appointed elder, has been teaching adult Sunday School using John Piper videos. He is also acting as the Sunday School superintendent for children's Sunday School. We no longer have a child, so we don't pay much attention to the curriculum that he is using. Some people seem to be infatuated with John Piper. Charles especially loves him. I, however, do not care much for him. I cannot, however, quite put my finger on why. One Sunday morning while watching a video, Mr. Piper, is talking about how everything is pre-determined in life and that we are just nails being used by the hammer of God. "Yes, I am a

Calvinist," He declares. *What's a Calvinist?* I have never heard that term.

As soon as we get home from church, I proceed to look up Calvinist. Whoa! I am shocked with what I find and more shocked to realize that something I had hoped to never encounter was in the midst of seemingly the most evangelical of churches. It is the belief that "God is the all-determining reality: that is, every single thing that happens has been rendered certain (ordained) by God because there is nothing God does not either directly or indirectly cause (including sin)."

For those of you reading this who have no idea, from this belief springs several principles outlined in Calvinism by an acronym -TULIP. T stands for Total depravity which most Christians would agree with. We are totally sinful and cannot save ourselves. What would be in dispute would be the belief that goes along with this that we are also totally unable to believe the Gospel message (dead) without God making us believe (or regenerating us before giving us salvation). U stands for Unconditional Election or the belief that God arbitrarily chose, through no action or attribute of the creature, before the world was formed, who He would give the gift of salvation to (predestination) and who He would "pass over" or damn to hell. L stands for Limited Atonement or the belief that Christ died only for those who God pre-elected and not for the whole world. I stands for Irresistible Grace or the belief that if God has chosen you to be one of His "elect" that you cannot resist His saving you. P stands for Perseverance of the Saints. In other words, since it is already pre-determined who will be saved, one's salvation (if so chosen) is guaranteed.[21]

As I study the chart on the internet source, I realize that I would probably fall mostly on the Arminian side though

I have never heard of this man either. I believe that we inherited the sin nature from Adam and Eve but not his guilt. We are incapable of being righteous on our own, but I believe we can respond to the grace that God extends to all of us.

I believe election is through Jesus Christ, the first Elect sometimes known as corporate election. The verse often quoted as a proof text, Ephesians 1:3-5 for predestination *3 Blessed be the God and Father of our Lord Jesus Christ, who has blessed us in Christ with every spiritual blessing in the heavenly places, 4 even as he* **chose us in him before the foundation of the world***, that we should be holy and blameless before him. In love 5 he predestined us for adoption as sons through Jesus Christ, according to the purpose of his will.*, I have never interpreted to say anything about predestination to salvation of individuals. God planned for Christ to be the salvation of mankind before the foundation of the world. Christ was the elect and it is through Him that we become the elect. The predestined in this verse has to do with once we have become one with Christ, we are then predestined to be considered adopted sons of God. We become His elect by responding to Jesus call.

I believe the atonement was for the sin of all men. I believe that God's grace is resistible. And I believe that there is assurance of salvation, but it is in relation to continued faithfulness. Several of these beliefs would not be strictly Arminian. It isn't until later that I realize that I have a truly Mennonite interpretation of scripture. But I do believe that 70-80% of those in TEFC, if closely questioned, would fall into the Arminian side of the spectrum.

After much reading and research, my mind and my faith are in a turmoil. Everything I have ever believed is being called into question. How is it possible that people can interpret the Bible in this manner? All I can see in the Calvinistic god is my father. A god who does not really love me. A stern hard-hearted being who uses his created beings as puppets only for His "glory." A god who is incomprehensible and schizophrenic. And a father who, apparently, was pre-destined to destroy his family with his pride and selfishness. I am left with so many questions and few answers. How can people interpret the Bible in so many ways? Who is right? Is there any way to escape from this pit of despair where I do not know what I believe and have no one that I can trust to make sense of all this? Every denomination interprets the Bible according to their brand. They all just make it say what they want it to say. Maybe all of this is just a big farce.

My hubby falls back into his prior obsession of believing he cannot possibly be saved if pre-destination is true. He knows his own heart and it is coated with black. He believes he cannot possibly be one of the "chosen." He cannot believe that God would purposely create millions of people for the sole purpose of sending them to hell. He is depressed, despondent, and angry. He has lost interest in living. We both feel betrayed by our pastor. We have trusted that he has been teaching us correctly from the Bible all these years. Why did we think that he had reversed paths after his earlier sermon on pre-destination some ten years prior? He has diligently been teaching these precepts silently all along and this is why the pastors and elders were all silent when we brought our observations to them at the elder interview meeting the prior year. And then it hits me like a bolt of lightning; *we are in the wrong church.* We have given over twenty years to a church that we do not believe is teaching what the Bible clearly teaches– that salvation is available to all.

Since it is within the early part of the year when the new schedules are developed, Gordon and I begin to pull out of most of what we have been involved in. This includes setting up for communion for me, helping in the nursery and greeting arrivals for both of us, and ushering and running the sound system for Gordon. I have already committed to be the treasurer for another year so there is not much I can do about that, but I determine to make a calculated withdrawal from this position by the end of 2015. There used to be a joke among the leadership that if the Farmers ever stopped being involved in everything that there is obviously a problem. It is not so funny now that it has happened, but it does not seem to cause anyone to stop and reflect or be alarmed. Being so involved in everything means we cannot just silently drift out the door and disappear like so many others do. To add to our confusion and consternation, Erin, our daughter announces that she wants to get married in September 2016 at Truth Evangelical Free Church. I don't know if we can hang on that long.

Gordon also turns down a request to sit on a reconvened building committee. The closure of the sale of the land to Kwik Trip is completed as planned in February 2015. The actual buying of the steel building that was approved was delayed by the elder team to make sure that the closure actually went forward. This decision to hold off on buying was made after several episodes of the land purchase being delayed and talk of a possible total falling through. When the Elder chairman calls to finally make the purchase of the steel building, it has just been sold to someone else after being for sale for five years. So, it is back to doing what should have been done in the first place – analyzing all the needs, costs, and options of an addition before plowing ahead.

With the steel building gone, attention turns to working out a deal with the gentleman that originally sold the church the land to build on. After negotiating most of the summer, an agreement is reached to buy 1.62 acres adjoining the south side of the property for $40,500. Step one has been completed in the process for an addition. We now have the land to build upon.

∞∞∞∞

Biblical Counseling training has been an ongoing aspiration of the leadership. Pastor Travis has been counseling using this program for a couple of years. In 2014, the church had hired the youth pastor who filled in after the sexual abuse case in 2002 to provide Biblical Counseling two days a week. In mid-June of 2015, this gentleman has a stroke and is unable to continue with the counseling. The church continues with their plan to send and pay for thirteen people to attend Biblical Counseling training in the summer. This is something I had indicated my interest in, but I am not surprised when I am not asked to participate. I have come to be seen as "broken." Gordon and I sense that we are no longer seen as part of the exclusive inner "spiritual" circle that has developed in this church. We are left to swim alone in a sea of doubt, anger, and confusion.

∞∞∞∞

Vacation Bible School is approaching again at TEFC. The last three years, Truth has partnered with the Church of Christ at their building for VBS. Gordon has helped with the decorating there, but it has not been the same. This year, the Church of Christ has decided to send their kids to camp instead of hosting VBS. This means that Truth must again put on their own Bible School. Gordon does agree to be in charge of the decorating. The theme is Son Sparks Labs. Fifty to sixty kids enjoy skits, songs, Bible stories, and science experiments each evening – all designed to point them to the gospel. Gordon designs and builds a giant marble run that loops around the perimeter of the church before shooting the balls down various slides. He uses pool balls instead of the marbles because they are larger. The balls start out on a lift that must be cranked to lift them up one by one to the run. After making their way to the front of the church and around, they return to fall through a series of different runs with different features before finally cycling down a funnel. It is a hit with the kids as usual. Gordon enjoys the bright smiles and excitement on the children's faces. It is the bright spot in our year.

∞∞∞∞

In the fall of 2015, the new associate pastor, Joshua, has started to teach during the Sunday School hour about the covenants between man and God throughout the Bible. He trades off intermittently with Charles. In October, Charles strays into some territory that sets off protest from several people. First, I have noticed that he brings into his teaching the idea that "God loves himself so much. If he didn't he would be practicing idolatry." I find this to be a strange circular argument that really serves no purpose. But this is not the only eccentric teaching. Somehow the topic of "are babies saved?" is raised.

"I believe babies are sinners like the rest of us," insists one man, "If you have any children at all you know they are sinners from day one. Contrary to what people say, I don't think there is any age of accountability," he finishes.

"You are right," agrees Charles, "The Bible does not say anywhere that babies or miscarried children go to heaven. It is for them like the rest of us. If God has pre-chosen them to be saved, they go to heaven. Otherwise, I don't think so."

I can't quite believe what I am hearing. All I can think is, telling someone who has just lost a baby that their child is in hell would be a disaster. Besides, how does that fit into the practice of adult baptism by faith? Very young children are not capable of accepting Christ by faith. So where does that leave all the children who are too young to make a confession of faith? Of course, if one believes everyone is pre-destined, I guess it doesn't make much difference. Come to think of it, a true Calvinist believes in infant baptism and that makes sense under the rationale that one can't change the outcome anyway.

Several people, me included, bring our concerns to the chairman of the elder board.

"Would you be willing to talk to Charles personally? That is the Biblical mandate – to talk to the person one-on-one first."

"Yes, I can talk to him. I don't have a problem with that."

Charles is too busy that Sunday to talk with me or the next couple of Sundays, so I give him a book to read, *Chosen but Free* by Norman Geisler. Before I am actually able to have a one-on-one conversation with him, he addresses the church to clarify his position. The congregation is encouraged by the pastor to give him grace.

He quotes I Corinthians 7:14 *"For the unbelieving husband is made holy because of his wife, and the unbelieving wife is made holy because of her husband. Otherwise your children would be unclean, but as it is, they are holy."* Through the use of this verse as a proof text, he makes his case that babies who are born to Christian parents go to heaven if they die. *Oh Please!*

Feeling somewhat snarky and being unable to accept that he actually believes this, I send him an e-mail, "How do I kindly say that I am not sure that your answer today scored any points for you or the Kingdom, so I thought you might want to read the article referenced below by John MacArthur." In it he says, "All children who die before they reach the *condition* (not age) of accountability by which they convincingly understand their sin and corruption and embrace the Gospel by faith are graciously saved eternally by God through the work of Jesus Christ."

There is no hesitation in Charles response, "Thank you for the article by John MacArthur. However, it appears we are not making progress to be reconciled on your concerns. Please let me know when you and Gordon are available within the next week or two. Pastor Travis and I would like to meet with you in person to make sure we are doing everything we can to avoid further miscommunication on this topic, and any other areas of concern."

Now I am disturbed. What is all this business about not making progress? Charles hasn't even made an attempt to talk to me personally. I agreed to talk to him personally, not in a group with the pastor present to side with him and make sure his position is validated. And why are they pulling my husband into this? Is this one of those complementarian expectations that a woman has to have her man to keep her under submission? Gordon does not want to talk to anyone. He is already beaten down and demoralized by this betrayal of beliefs. This whole situation has gone from bad to worse.

Reluctantly, we agree to meet with Charles, Pastor Travis, and another elder I have asked to join us. Gordon and I are defensive, guarded, and feel trapped in what seems like another trip to the principal's office for rebuke and remediation. The conversation involves many aspects of our differing beliefs but several things that are said solidifies for us that Pastor Travis is distinctly Calvinistic, an issue that we were not totally sure of before.

"The Bible says that God loved Jacob and hated Esau in Romans 9:13," Pastor Travis declares as evidence that God pre-determines to love some people and hate others. I am puzzled and bewildered by this logic as the Bible also says, "if any one comes to me and does not hate his father and mother... he cannot be my disciple." Luke 14:26 and we don't take that to mean we should actually hate our family. But then I think, maybe God did tell Rebecca in Genesis that he would hate the one and love the other. But when I look up Genesis 25:23 later, it says, "Two nations are in your womb, and two peoples from within you will be separated; one people will be stronger than the other, and the older will serve the younger." It says nothing about hating one and loving the other. Finally, I realize that the verse quoted in Romans actually comes from Malachi 1:2-3 where the prophet is talking about the nation that resulted from Jacob and the nation that came out of Esau. One followed God and one did not. The statement has nothing to do with the persons of Jacob and Esau. Confusion whirls around in my brain that our seminary trained pastor cannot see this small misinterpretation that is being used as a proof text.

"Who killed Jesus?" is the next thought-provoking question thrown our way. I pause. How do I answer this without them saying, "Got you?" I don't have an answer for him that I can spit out immediately, but I don't think it is a simple "God did it" or "Men did it." God in his omnipotence and sovereignty knew what the culture and political situation of the time would be when He would send Jesus to earth. He knew there would be men happy to betray Jesus and to desire his crucifixion. Yes, it was in the plan of God from before the world began to send His Son for our sins, but he did not make any of the men who participated in Christ's death do it. Even Judas was not pre-condemned. He could have received forgiveness if he had sought it rather than hanging himself.

"At the least, you must believe that regeneration comes before faith?" Pastor Travis peers at us questioningly. I can only shake my head back and forth. No, I don't believe that. "How do you explain then the conversion of Paul? God regenerated his heart before he had faith."

My mouth must be hanging open as I stare at Travis. "Most of us are not hit over the head by God with a blinding light so I don't think one can generalize any conclusions based on Saul's conversion." After all, God had a special assignment for Saul and he needed to get his attention. Saul obviously was not making the choice God wanted him to. Otherwise he would not have needed to use extraordinary means. If the belief is true that God regenerates the heart before one can believe, why didn't he just regenerate Saul's heart without the hitting him over the head.

"Have you talked to Pastor Joshua?" I address Travis, "It doesn't seem like from his preaching that he is Calvinistic." Travis gazes at me but does not answer. My stomach sinks to my feet. So they are all of this persuasion. We are in the minority.

We are more confused and upset after this meeting. It is now blatantly obvious to us that everyone, with the exception of one man, in the leadership has been swayed by the Calvinistic system of theology. It is what they listen to, what they read, what they convince themselves of. We feel shamed for believing that it is a choice to accept Christ's salvation. We feel like second-class Christians who are undeserving of God's blessings and acceptance. Gordon is totally lost in shame, failure, and convinced he is not good enough to be one of the "chosen."

Besides concern for my husband, my overall concern is how this creep towards focusing on the Calvinistic side of how we come to salvation will eventually affect the unity of the church. The Evangelical Free Church of America does not have any statement of belief on this topic. There is nothing in the ten statements of the Free Church belief that incorporates the first four tenants of Calvinism. The EFC, as a body, believes this teaching is not an essential and people should not split over it. The problem is the person teaching, then cannot be fervently fixated on this position if they are not going to cause division, considering that many in the congregation do not hold this belief. I believe my duty is to caution the leadership to be aware of what positions they hold and how it may affect the church as a whole. I begin a campaign with books and articles to try to show the pastor wherein Calvinism is wrong in how it is using proof texts to create this systematic theology and not considering the whole context of the Bible and the gospel. I write to Pastor Travis and the elders in November 2015,

I come with a humble heart, so I hope you don't misread my intentions, but I would like to share with all of you some articles that I hope you will graciously read and thoughtfully research and consider in the light of God's Word. I challenge you to go back to the original text, the context of the various scriptures being used to support pre-destination to heaven or hell, and the overall character of God within the context of his Word. I am not in any way smart enough to take on learned men, but I do understand that the gospel is for all mankind and God's word was written so even children could understand the gospel message. Maybe we are making it way more complicated than God ever intended.

I have no illusion that I am ever going to change minds, but God has put this burden on my heart and I will follow His leading by sharing it with you. I hope you can be open enough to at least read the attached papers. Thanks. Amanda

As I study more about this topic and this trend in the church, I learn that I have been sitting under the preaching of Calvinism for a long time but not recognizing it primarily because of the redefining of Biblical terms. I have only vaguely been sensing that something is not right. Pastor Travis preaches constantly about the "sovereignty" of God. I believe in the sovereignty of God so what is the problem? "Sovereignty" to Travis means "divine determination" or the principle that God pre-determines everything about our life and that of everyone in the world. "Sovereignty" to me means that God is in complete control, but he has withheld his total power for now in order to allow man to have free will or the ability to make choices about life and about worshipping Him.

"Human depravity" under Calvinism is defined as the condition of being "dead in your transgressions and sins" Ephesians 2:1 with dead being defined as "rigor mortis" dead or unable to do anything. Therefore, God has to regenerate the person before they can have faith. In my view, this is an incorrect interpretation of "dead" in the Bible. In Genesis 2:17 God tells Adam and Eve, "but from the tree of the knowledge of good and evil you shall not eat, for in the day that you eat from it you will surely die." Did they become "rigor mortis" dead when they ate of the tree? No, they were separated from God and eventually did physically die but even then, dead means a separation from those on earth. In Luke 15:24, the Father in the story of the prodigal son says, "For this son of mine was dead and is alive again! He was lost and is found! So they began to celebrate." The son was capable of coming home to his father. He was not "rigor mortis" dead and his father did not go get him.

Another example of the changing of meaning that occurs to assist the Calvinistic theological system in meshing together is the redefining of the word "all." The many verses that talk about Jesus dying for "all" are redefined to mean He died for "all the elect." These redefinitions are subtle and often not verbalized but they change the underlying premise for believing what one believes.

I approach different people in the congregation to get a feel for how others view this Calvinism teaching. 80% of the people do not know what I am talking about. "What's Calvinism?" is the most common response I get. Other responses include:

"I don't try to figure out such things. I let the pastors study those issues."

"Of course, I believe in pre-destination. My daughter is so mean, I know she is pre-destined to hell."

"I am not going to change churches at our age no matter what happens. I know what I believe."

Wow, no wonder I feel like we are alone in this struggle.

About this time also, I come across a book by Austin Fisher entitled, *Young Restless No Longer Reformed: Black Holes, Love, and a Journey In and Out of Calvinism.* The book is thought provoking, easy to read, and helps me think through the issues of this resurgent system of theology that has been plastered in front of my face. I am so excited about the book, I buy a dozen and begin to hand them out to close friends in the church who seem interested in this topic that is just coming to the surface.

Chapter 17 Grooming the Church for More Desired Changes

P art of a letter I write to one of the elders displays my emotional state at this time.

I am struggling with what to do with my mounting frustration of just being brushed aside (sometimes not even responded to) when I try to share the things that I sense will result in heartache and failure in the future life of the church. If I had to use one word to describe how I feel as a member of the church and of the Administrative Council, that word would be "powerless." For me, the response to sharing one's insights is met in one of two ways. If I take the time to write things down, the response here in the last year has just been to not respond at all or it could lead to an invitation to share face to face with the leadership. And I have backed away from doing that because verbally sharing concerns results in Travis (instead of listening and carefully considering the opposite position) instantly justifying his (and supposedly the leaderships?) position with a righteous sounding response that may or may not be the only Biblical response. What was once a congregational run church is no longer that way. It has slowly and stealthily (like the frog put in water and heated slowly until he is cooked) become a pastor run church – just the structure the founding fathers were trying to prevent.

I feel a lot like Jeremiah in the old testament must have felt. He went to the king with the message God instructed him to give and the king had him thrown in a muddy cistern. [Jeremiah 38:6] I, and another woman, who has the gift of discernment both believe that the leadership is no longer following the Holy Spirit in the decisions that they are making.

∞∞∞∞

Throughout the year of 2015, Pastor Travis has been preaching on "Rediscovering the Church." There are sermons on the God-Centered Church, The Gospel-Defined Church, Gospel Community, Male Leadership in the Church, Spiritual Leadership, and the Church as a New Covenant Community. I do not see until I look back that these are specifically chosen topics to lead the congregation into the proposed plan to be presented in the coming year. At the annual meeting for 2015, Pastor Travis talks about Biblical Counseling and church discipline, "the heart of the counselee determines which path they chose to take: counseling or church discipline." So the Biblical counseling program has not only been implemented to help those seeking help but to try to change the behavior of those who are deemed by leadership to not be following Biblical principles. The belief that the church has the rightful authority to put pressure on people to follow what the church has determined is Biblically mandated, I find troubling. Pastor Travis's goal for the coming year is to "continue to grow as a church that is grounded in our identity as God-centered, Christ-exalting, and Gospel defined. May God continue to shape the beauty of true transformative Gospel-Community among us..." He concludes with again informing the congregation that "our elder team is implementing what we call our shepherding plan. This is one attempt for us to get more connected with each family in our body so that we can have better communication with you, and more importantly, so that we can pray more strategically for you and be available to offer shepherding or counsel as necessary."[22] Nothing in this plan moving forward sounds particularly unbiblical or dangerous. Other than the relevant aspect of the elders, who have full-time jobs, not having time for such a time-consuming strategy, we are naïve about the intentions of the pastors or what this all might mean. I know nothing about the "Shepherding plans" in other churches that have led to spiritual abuse in their congregations.

∞∞∞∞

So what is the red flag in regards to "shepherding?" The Shepherding Movement emerged in 1974. In 1970, a group of four Charismatic Bible teachers met together - Bernard (Bob) Mumford, ordained through the Assemblies of God; Derek Prince, another Pentecostal; Don Basham, an ordained Disciples of Christ minister; and Charles Simpson, originally a Southern Baptist. The four decided to mutually submit to one another and to hold each other accountable, and it was through New Wine, their church magazine, that the peculiar teachings of the Shepherding Movement were emphasized and promoted: authority, submission, discipleship, commitment in covenant relationships, loyalty, pastoral care, and spiritual covering. The four Shepherds taught and practiced a style of leadership that they called "shepherding." They used this term to describe attempts to control the private lives of their members. In neo-discipleship groups, there is absolute submission to the shepherd. Everyone is submitted in a regimented authoritarian chain of command. Someone is between you and God at all times.[23]

Most of this original movement has died out due to a proliferation of spiritual abuse. In her book, *Twisted Scriptures: Breaking Free From Churches that Abuse*, Mary Alice Chrnalogar talks about the resurgence of "discipleship/shepherding groups." "The foundation of the discipleship movement is the authority of the discipler. What distinguishes discipleship relationships from the typical relationship between a pastor and the flock is that the discipler is granted a significantly greater authority to guide the directions and decisions of the disciple... Non-controlling churches generally follow more accurately the Scripture and only teach trusting in God, having faith in God, having loyalty to God, and imitating the life and virtues of Jesus or the virtues of Jesus in people."[24]

Matthew 23: 2-4 says "The teachers of the law and the Pharisees sit in Moses' seat. [3] So you must be careful to do everything they tell you. But do not do what they do, for they do not practice what they preach. [4] They tie up heavy, cumbersome loads and put them on other people's shoulders, but they themselves are not willing to lift a finger to move them." (NIV) Jesus made it plain that we are to honor the teachers and to trust the message but not to follow them as they place men in bondage with their rules.

∞∞∞∞

It is also around this time that I realize the translation of the Bible being used by the pastors and leadership is the ESV. When did that change occur, I ask Gordon? When Pastor Travis first came, he was using the NASB. Gordon went out and bought a NASB so that he could follow along in the translation being read from the pulpit and during Bible study in elder meetings. Now we realize that they have quietly moved to the ESV as the translation the leaders are using. The ESV was translated primarily by a committee overseen by Wayne Grudem. Mr. Gruden served as the General Editor of the ESV from 2005–2008. Wayne Grudem is also known for his systematic theology book, *Systematic Theology: An Introduction to Biblical Doctrine.* This translation and all his other works are written through the eyes of a key person in the Neo-Calvinist /Complementarian movements.[25]

Chapter 18 More Calvinism Discussion

As we move closer to the new year, I am devastated by the total loss of faith of my husband and the position we find ourselves in. We go to church, but it means nothing. I am not sure how we became misfits in a church we have supported for twenty-five years but it is a lonely place to be. One day after Pastor Joshua teaches Sunday School, I approach him in tears. My world is falling apart, and I am sad and angry all at the same time. We talk in the entry for a few minutes and then agree to meet in his office later in the week.

Pursuant to our conversation, I attach an article, *Why I am no Longer a Calvinist* by Tim Pierce, to an e-mail and send it. I find it convincing and interesting to read and hope that Joshua will take the time to read it and offer his thoughts.

The most often voiced justifications for Calvinism that I hear is that "God is God," "God can do whatever he wants," and "we all deserve hell so any one God choses to save is receiving his grace and mercy." First, the overall problem with the Calvinistic viewpoint, as I see it, is that the premise from which the whole doctrine is built on is faulty. I do agree that "God is God" and "God can do whatever he wants." I also agree that if God decides to save some and send others to hell that is his prerogative. The problem with all of this is that it is not the God that He reveals himself to be in the Bible or in His creation. God is not a God of randomness. Everything he has created has intricate order and purpose in his creation. He tells us who He is in His Word and what His expectations of us are. Obviously, we can't live up to them without his help (Jesus Christ) but he does tell us what we need to do to receive that help and salvation – believe. When the attributes of God are all taken together, I do not see a heartless God who randomly chooses some for salvation and others not, simply because he can. He could but he doesn't. It is a strange circular argument to say that since all of us deserve hell (of course, we do) that the belief that He randomly chooses to save some somehow makes it fit with who God has revealed Himself to be. This would go back to the question of "Why did God make man?" I, based on the scriptures, believe God made man to have a relationship with Him and he wants his creatures to **willingly** serve and worship Him. If this is not so, why does God spend so much of the old testament telling His people to "follow me," "obey me," "serve me," "keep my commands." We truly do not understand the depth and the magnitude of God. Therefore, we have trouble conceptualizing that God created creatures in His own image who he allows to choose whether they will love and worship Him and is still able to sovereignly be in control of the whole world. My God is way bigger than the one who can only make things work out by having puppets and robots.

These have always been my beliefs and I used to think that I had my faith and my relationship to God within His plan all figured out. Now Pastor Joshua begins to throw strange concepts at me.

"The Fall was always part of God's plan from the beginning," Joshua declares. "God let Adam and Eve fall purposefully. Did he make them do it? No, they wanted to after Satan's tempting. Were they free to confound the plans of God by obeying him? I think not. Texts like Acts 3:23 *"Anyone who does not listen to him will be completely cut off from their people"* make this very plain. How else could Jesus have died without sinners to die for? Jesus death was not a reaction to what God knew of Adam and Eve's disobedience. It was the plan **from the beginning.**"

I am shocked by these assertations to say the least, "What a bizarre thing to say – that if Adam and Eve had obeyed God they would not have been following God's plan. There is nothing in Acts 3:23 that says that or anywhere else in the Bible. Also, if Adam and Eve were not 'free' to obey God and 'confound His plan' then they and us are not morally responsible for our actions. One must have a free choice in order to be morally responsible. If there is no free choice, then God is responsible for all evil in the world as well as the good. I know you will say both are true. God 'planned for them to do it' and man is still responsible, but both CANNOT be true. Free choice is necessary for moral responsibility to be present.

God knew that His creation would sin, so having no sinners to die for would not be a problem. Foreknowledge (all knowing), however, does not constitute a pre-determined outcome. You said that it was God's plan that man would fall in the Garden of Eden (and by inference that God is responsible for evil). I challenge you to show me Biblical proof for that statement. Saying that God 'planned from all eternity to redeem a people for himself' does not rise to the level of Biblical proof that the fall had to occur. There is a huge leap in logic there that does not necessarily follow through to your conclusion. Take for example, as your children learned to walk, you knew that they would fall down multiple times. Does that mean that you made them fall down? Of course not." I assert.

"I think it is fitting for us to ascribe ultimate causality for all things (good and evil) to the good purposes of God." Continues Joshua. "Why do I say so? Because there are several examples in the Bible that indicate so. Job does not say that God allowed or caused his possessions and family to be taken away but that God, himself, took them away. Job 1: 21 'The LORD gave, and the LORD has taken away; blessed be the name of the LORD. In all this, Job did not sin or charge God with wrong.' And in Genesis 45:5-8, Joseph too ascribes the evil that happened to him as being planned by the sovereign hand of God. '⁵ And now, do not be distressed and do not be angry with yourselves for selling me here, because it was to save lives that God sent me ahead of you. ⁶ For two years now there has been famine in the land, and for the next five years there will be no plowing and reaping. ⁷ But God sent me ahead of you to preserve for you a remnant on earth and to save your lives by a great deliverance. ⁸ "So then, it was not you who sent me here, but God. He made me father to Pharaoh, lord of his entire household and ruler of all Egypt.'"

"Saying that Job's statement of 'the Lord giveth and the Lord taketh away' proves that God planned for the evil that fell upon Job does not hold up to the conclusion. This was an example of God **allowing** a man to suffer at the hands of Satan to prove to Satan that Job would be faithful to God. God did not make that statement. Job did, and it proves nothing about God's preplanning and his being the author of evil. Job saying that "God gives, and God takes away" was his belief about the situation and not necessarily God's. God allowed it yes. Job's calamity was Satan's plan which God allowed to make a point to Satan. The same is true of Joseph. 'It was not you who sent me here, but God' were Joseph's words meant to comfort his frightened brothers who knew they had done wrong by selling him into slavery in Egypt. Does this mean that God was so small that he couldn't get Joseph to Egypt without making his brothers sin? I don't think so. But God does use their sin for good."

"Consider the language of Deuteronomy 32:39," Joshua continues as if this seals the inference he is making, "See now that I, even I, am he, and there is no god beside me: I kill, and I make alive; I wound, and I heal: neither is there any that can deliver out of my hand."

This verse is spoken in the context of God's people pursuing after other gods and I see this statement like that of a father who says to his teenage son, "I am the father. I control what comes in and out of my house. I can withhold the car and your allowance. I make the decisions." This, however, does not mean that the father or God has predetermined what will happen. The child has a choice that effects the consequences.

"I would like to ask you one last question," I conclude. "Did God plan that the devil and his angels would rise up in rebellion against Him - that that was part of his pre-determined plan too?"

"Yes," he responds, "the rebellion of Satan against God was part of the pre-determined plan."

My brain is spinning. I don't even know where to go with this. "Your response about the devil has no basis. There is nothing in the Bible that says Satan's rebellion against God was planned by God. That is pure speculation on your part. It just fits nicely into the logic of the Calvinist system. Saying that all of evil is a part of God's plan creates a whole new set of problems for you and me. If murder, rape etc etc

143

are all part of God's plan, then I have no idea how you explain that one to suffering people and why would I want to be involved with a God like that. Why then, too, do you get involved in the situations of the world? Why are you involved in the political caucus? It is apparently God's plan that Donald Trump be, at least, the republican candidate. You are opposing God's plan by trying to have someone else be the candidate. Why are you and your wife boycotting Target? It apparently is God's plan that man will sin more and more and nothing you do is going to change that. So you see where I am going?"

Many thoughts roll around in my head. What happens to people in life who make no choices, who wait for God to work out things in their life by no action? It works somewhat if you are a Christian to just get up each morning and go to whatever job jumps out in front of you. But it is a totally different matter if you are a drunkard or a drug addict and you believe that is God's plan for your life or more likely, your destiny. After all, if it is pre-determined, that is the case. And does God pre-determine that some people will commit suicide? That doesn't even make sense. Why would one work so hard to teach one's children about God and pray for them to accept Christ if one truly believes that salvation is granted by God randomly and only as he chooses. Finally, why pray at all if it makes no difference?

"I want to ask you one last question," Joshua focuses on the issue of moral responsibility. "Why do you so strongly insist that 'one must have a free choice in order to be morally responsible'?"

"Why do I so strongly insist on this point?" I shoot back. "Probably for the same reason that you insist that God cannot be sovereign if he allows man to freely choose whether to worship Him or not. We have two very different views of what God's purpose was in creating man. One view sees God's dealing with man as a cat who plays with a mouse for the sole purpose of showing the man that He (God) can do whatever he (God) wills and this somehow is supposed to glorify Him. If man has no choice, he is being punished for behavior he has no control over and I don't know that God. A God who is just, loving, fair and everything else I believe God to be will not randomly select some to love him and create others randomly and, with nothing within their control, for hell. I believe God created man because he wanted man to choose willingly to worship Him and to honor Him. Evil is the consequence of man's choice to sin, but God's overall desire is to love us like a Father and for us to love him like we want our children to love us. That is why He sent Jesus to be the redemption for us. We were created in His image for a reason. God desires that none should perish. There are many verses in the Bible that indicate that salvation is open to all who choose to accept that free gift.

I John 2:2 *He (Christ) is the atoning sacrifice for our sins, and not only for ours but also for the sins of the* **whole world***.*

Romans 10:13 *For* **whosoever** *shall call upon the name of the Lord shall be saved.*

John 5:24 *Truly, truly, I say to you, he who hears My word, and believes Him who sent Me, has eternal life, and does not come into judgement, but has passed out of death into life.*

Mark 16:16 **Whoever** *believes and is baptized will be saved, but whoever does not believe will be condemned.*

I John 5: 11-13 *And the testimony is this, that God has given us eternal life, and this life is in His Son. He who has the Son has the life; he who does not have the Son of God does not have the life. These things I have written to you who believe in the name of the Son of God, so that you may know that you have eternal life.*

I John 1:9 If we confess our sins, He is faithful and righteous to forgive us our sins and to cleanse us from all unrighteousness.

Romans 10:9 Because, if you confess with your mouth that Jesus is Lord and believe in your heart that God raised him from the dead, you will be saved.

*Revelation 3:20 Behold, I stand at the door and knock. If **anyone** hears my voice and opens the door, I will come in to him and eat with him and he with me*

John 1:12 But as many as received Him, to them He gave the right to become children of God, even to those who believe in His name

John 6:35 And Jesus said unto them, I am the bread: he that cometh to me shall never hunger; and he that believeth on me shall never thirst.

John 3: 16-17 For God so loved the world that he gave his one and only Son, that whoever believes in him shall not perish but have eternal life. For God did not send his Son into the world to condemn the world, but to save the world through Him.

"The fact that these verses conflict with Calvinists interpretation of certain other verses should cause us all to pause and wonder if we are interpreting everything correctly. Maybe I need to ask you to define for me your meaning of the words 'plan,' and 'sovereign?'" I conclude. "All I can say Joshua is that you are destroying the faith of my husband and I with what you have brought into our church with the Calvinistic system of belief. Maybe you are totally right. I don't know. But I think you need to be careful in how dogmatic you are in your position. Satan has started to whisper, 'Maybe none of this is true. Everyone who reads the Bible has a different interpretation and they can't all be right.' I, in the final analysis, cannot support a church who believes that God is the author of evil and that 'salvation' is only for a few pre-selected individuals. I am not saying this in an angry hostile manner. I am distressed to the point I no longer sleep at night and have not for the last six months. This craziness goes around and around in my head as I try to make some kind of sense of your teaching and how it fits with the real world and our everyday lives. And the problem is, it doesn't fit."

Amidst the various passionate discussions, I have with Pastor Joshua, he directs a question at me one day. "Will you help me teach a Sunday School class on Arminianism/Calvinism as a debate? I would present the side of Calvinism and you could debate for the side of Arminianism. It might not happen until the spring of 2018 so you would have plenty of time to prepare."

"Oh no," I reply, "I am like Moses – I can't speak eloquently."

I would be the loser in any debate with Joshua. He is confident, almost arrogant. He behaves like a court lawyer. His answers pop out without any effort. Besides, I am at a huge disadvantage taking the side opposing the pastor's view. Who is going to listen to the theologically uneducated woman? I sense he can already smell victory though there is a part of me that feels someone has to fight for God's reputation.

"We will probably be gone by then anyway," I finish.

Chapter 19 Seeking A Church Statement of Conciliation

In mid-December 2015, I write a letter to the elders regarding the Arminian/Calvinism issue, seeking to have the elders acknowledge to the congregation that these two positions on salvation exist, first of all, and to assure everyone that neither position will be affirmed as the official one of the congregation. The Evangelical Free Church of America has what is called the "significance of silence" position regarding "non-essential" issues and I am requesting that Truth adhere to this. So what is the "significance of silence?" According to Greg Strand, EFCA executive director of theology and credentialing, and member of the Board of Ministerial Standing as well as the Spiritual Heritage Committee, the "significance of silence" stipulates that "one is privileged to hold either view (of a non-essential issue) and still be a member in good standing of a local congregation. It is only in a strict adherence to this principle of freedom, respect for the views of others, and restraint in teaching one view as though it is the official view of the denomination when it is actually silent on the subject, that this unity can be maintained."[26]

Dear Elders:
I would like to address everyone one more time at the risk of being considered obnoxious. I am sorry if I am pressing this issue

too hard, but I feel it is an extremely important issue to address and take a position on. As you all know, Gordon and I have come to realize that TEFC has shifted over the last dozen years from being primarily an Arminian/Wesleyan believing group of people to containing not only two Calvinistic/ Reformed pastors but having also other members who hold the more Calvinistic position. I did not understand for a long time what it was that I was seeing. I only knew that it was not what we believed. After much study and research, I think I now understand that there are two very different views on issues such as pre-destination, atonement, election, human depravity etc. My understanding is the Evangelical Free Church of America takes the position that these differences are not "essentials" of the faith and should not divide us. When Gordon and I met with Travis, Charles, and the other elder, most of the time was spent in trying to make us see the errors of our position. One of Travis's comments was that we "must" believe that "regeneration comes before faith". If we believe that, all the other five points of the TULIP must be essentials too because they all go together.

I have attached a paper that outlines the position of the Evangelical Free Church of America of which Truth is a member. My question is, "Is there really room for both views in this church? Joshua told me that TEFC is not changing their statement of faith but from a practical operating standpoint, they already have. It is just not in writing. We feel marginalized and like we no longer measure up from a spiritual standpoint since we do not embrace the Calvinistic viewpoint. Yes, we can and may leave for this reason but getting rid of the Farmers is not going to solve what I see as a looming problem that has the potential to split the church. The underlying issue here is "Can TEFC affirm those on both sides of the issue?" and allow into leadership and decisions about the direction of the church those who do NOT believe the Calvinistic perspective. The town of

Corinth does not contain a lot of Calvinistic people so sooner or later Truth needs to address this issue if it hopes to grow.

My belief is Truth needs to affirm both positions or at least acknowledge that there are two different positions that have existed for 1600 years. Maybe adding it to the "significance of silence" category that EFCA talks about as a non-essential might be appropriate. Part of that would mean not always choosing teaching materials that are Calvinistic in their slant because that is what both pastors now are.

I am not trying to tell you what to do, at this point, because I, personally have already determined that I cannot remain long term in a church whose only choice of belief is the Calvinistic perspective. I just can't make that leap in turning my beliefs totally upside down after almost sixty years. Gordon is not prepared to deal with any more challenges to his faith right now, so I am writing this from me personally. I love the people here and would like to think that the leadership would choose and affirm the position of the EFCA as theirs here at Truth and accept as equal heirs of eternal life brothers and sisters who profess Christ but are not of the Calvinistic persuasion.

Respectfully and humbly submitted,
Amanda

I am hoping that my letter will be met with soft hearts and an acknowledgement from the leadership that they understand that there have been two positions on the soteriology of salvation for many years and that they accept that many people believe as we do and that that is OK at TEFC. That is all I am expecting. But the letter that comes back has some harsh punitive tones to it.

TEFC Elder Board

December 22, 2015

Dear Amanda,

On behalf of the elder board, we want you to know that we love you and have been praying for both you and Gordon in this trying season of your lives. We appreciate your taking the time to draft and submit your letter to the elders regarding an important doctrine with which you and Gordon have been struggling.

Above all, it is our desire that we stay faithful to the Scriptures as we lead and shepherd our whole flock. In this season, we believe that the highest priority for the Farmer family is one-on-one counseling with Gordon. While there is merit in discussing the doctrines involved with the Calvinist-Arminian debate, we agree that now is not the best time for public discourse on the matter. We hope this letter will help you understand why and how we made this decision. Though we may disagree, it is our desire that, wherever we may disagree on non-essential and preferential issues, you would see them – not as grounds for division- but as opportunities to humbly submit your judgement to ours.

In response to your letter you gave Monday, the elders have drafted these two points for you to review. Since these points are already public knowledge (available online or in our church's governing documents), we do not find it necessary to discuss or make any changes to our governing documents at this time.

In addition to supplying you with the points listed below, we would ask you to supply specific examples of the following cited in your letter:

Theological coercion: where Travis attempted to compel you to believe that "regeneration comes before faith" – something that Travis, Charles, and the other elder do not recall happening during your meeting.

Marginalization for your *theological* beliefs: per "We feel marginalized... since we do not embrace the Calvinistic perspective."
Both charges are significant and must be substantiated in light of our commitment to point 2.h & 2.1 (below)

Calvinism and the EFCA
The EFCA and TEFCA have wisely considered discourse surrounding Calvinism and Arminianism as non-essential for salvation and fellowship (between individuals and associated churches).
However, this doctrinal "silence" does not mean that Free Churches are in any way prohibited from holding a particular position within a church's leadership (either officially or unofficially).
Neither is TEFC obligated to affirm *both* positions in order to be compliant with the EFCA.
It does mean that the EFCA will *not* restrict denominational association from churches that hold to either a Calvinistic or Arminian perspective.

It also means that the EFCA *may* restrict denominational association from churches that *require* an affirmation of either Calvinism or Arminianism for church membership.

Calvinism and TEFC

There has never been an official statement regarding Calvinism and/or Arminianism. Thus, there has been no doctrinal change with regard to this issue since the church's founding.

All pastors/elders at TEFC are affirmed as men of good, moral character and sound, theological judgment by the body and have been entrusted to lead and shepherd the church.

Pastors/elders are required to fully affirm that which accords with and is not contrary to the positions expressed in the church's doctrinal statement.

Pastors/elders may hold doctrinal and philosophical beliefs that exist beyond but do not run contrary to the positions expressed in the church's doctrinal statement.

Furthermore, pastors/elders may teach various positions on different points of doctrine but are not to be compelled to affirm as true any position that runs contrary to their own beliefs.

Pastors/elders have the prerogative to lead according to their conviction; these convictions can and should impact the ethos and direction of TEFC.

Whatever perceived, non-essential, doctrinal shifts that have taken place over TEFC's history have been either owing to changes in leadership or reforms to the leadership's personal convictions and are not owing to any change in official church doctrine.

Anyone affirming either the Calvinistic or Arminian perspective is welcome to attend, seek membership, and be considered for church leadership at TEFC.

Pastors/elders do not compel members to believe or affirm anything more than the church's governing documents.

All members are free at any time to remove their membership or worship elsewhere for any reason whatsoever.

For clarifying questions regarding the specific content of this letter, you are free to respond directly to Pastor Joshua.

Please submit responses to (a) and (b) via our email thread.

Moving forward, we ask you direct all future questions and concerns regarding our position on either this doctrinal issue or other leadership decisions to Chairman of the Board.

In His service,
TEFC Elders

I am hurt and confused by the letter. The tone is not friendly, and I sense some undertones of needing to be firm with us. It is like they are trying to make us understand that we cannot manipulate and control the direction of the church and that if we stay, we need to be submissive. I ask myself why. Have we communicated that our intent is to override the elders and influence the church to go in a way that is not Biblical? Do they believe that we are trying to deliberately divide the church? That is not the case. I have only wanted the leadership to develop a plan to deal with differing beliefs in a manner that affirms each side and does not divide. Does the leadership not welcome the wisdom of those in the congregation who have been around for years and can see the changes that have occurred? Do they see us as simply being instigators of dissention? Why would the leadership take a position of "Though we may disagree, it is our desire that, wherever we may disagree on non-essential and preferential issues, you would see them – not as grounds for division – but as opportunities to humbly submit your judgment to ours." If they are "non-essential and preferential issues," why is it so important that we submit to the leadership's judgement on them? The Bible says, "But the people of Berea were more open-minded than those in Thessalonica, and gladly listened to the message. They searched the Scriptures day by day to check up on Paul and Silas' statements to see if they were really so —" Acts 17:11 Do they not believe that we should do this?

In response to their request for us to submit a response to (a) and (b), I send the following:

In response to (a) in Pastor Joshua's letter, Gordon and I did not request this meeting with Charles and Travis (I ask the other elder to join us) or in any way want it. I was the one that approached the elder chairman. and at his request, agreed to bring my concern directly to Charles. That was all I agreed to do so it has thrown me and Gordon into a confusing emotional and spiritual crisis we did not sign up for. What really was the purpose of the meeting? We saw it as an attempt to convince us that we are the ones in error and not Charles? Maybe that doesn't rise to the level of theological coercion, but it sure felt like a meeting to exhort us in the "right" way. Having said that, my words have been changed into something I did not say. I did not state that Travis attempted to compel us to believe that "regeneration comes before faith." What I said was "when

Gordon and I met with Travis, the elder chairman, and Charles, most of the time was spent in trying to make us see the errors of our position. One of Travis's comments was that we "must" believe that "regeneration comes before faith." That has a totally different connotation and feeling than what you have written as my charge. He wasn't compelling us to believe anything at that point. I believe he was stating that he believed this point was essential to his beliefs and those who would desire to lead this church. That is a telling statement. And my husband does remember this statement, so I have no way to explain why the other three are saying they don't remember this happening.

In response to (b), "marginalization" probably is not the right word. "A fall from grace" would be a better characterization of what has occurred in regards to our position in the church. How can we not feel that we are somehow not spiritual enough now for any service in this church? Three years ago, Gordon was removed from being the building committee chairman because someone who was seen to have more gifts came along. Then he was removed from elder consideration because of a "lack of faith" so this is just a continuing of the trend. I truly believe that the withholding of office for my husband was a result of feelings toward me. He had done nothing deserving of being passed over and it has resulted in a crisis of faith that has only been accentuated by the recent revelation of the importance of Calvinistic beliefs which we do not hold.

In conclusion, one of Joshua's points was that "all members are free at any time to remove their membership or worship elsewhere for any reason whatsoever." That is an interesting thing to say as Travis and the elders have encouraged commitment to the local body and we have committed our lives in all ways to this church for 25 years, so it feels like a slap in the face to read, "feel free to leave whenever."

I have grown very depressed over the last few months and have lost interest in all aspects of life as there seems to be no purpose. I struggle to function every day. Truth was our family and it feels like we are no longer regarded as people whose life experience and wisdom are valuable to the life of the church. Anytime I open my mouth, it seems like I am met with the assumption that I am proud and trying to manipulate things.

A few years later in 2018, I have an e-mail conversation with Greg Strand after he publishes the article ***Navigating Theological Differences and Maintaining Unity:*** *How churches throughout the EFCA live out the "significance of silence"* on the Evangelical Free Church website. I respond to his article in a comment:

This article drew my attention as "Soteriological Essentials" and the "Significance of Silence in the EFCA" is a topic that is close to my heart. I was especially interested in learning about what the EFCA says about how a local church can have both Arminian and Calvinistic beliefs in it and thrive. Greg Strand's statement that the "significance of silence" does not mean that we will not talk about these issues, or that this is not a lowest common denominator type of approach but one of "robust dialogue without dividing" interests me. Do you really think that in a local church there can be "robust dialogue" without a wedge being driven between those who are of opposing views?

Is such a thing even possible I wonder? Can two factions who are passionate about their positions actually live together in the same church? If the Free Church thinks this is possible, there should be some kind of counseling or help for the church attempting this. I personally don't know what that looks like, but I do know there has to be an official acceptance of both sides and attempts to respect those who do not hold your position. Whatever position the leadership holds cannot be the only one taught and those on the other side viewed as lesser Christians in need of enlightenment. Teaching one side without educating and informing the congregation I also see as less than honest.

Though Dr. Strand responds graciously to my comments, I am somewhat disappointed with the answer and realize that there is no assistance for those such as us who find ourselves in a minority position through nothing we have done. After all, we are not the ones who have changed our belief system and convictions.

You will find flaws and imperfections in any and all churches. And yet, all biblically faithful churches have a biblical ideal of what the church ought to be. Every church is committed to the biblical ideal and yet lives with the real. There are no exceptions. So even though we in the EFCA articulate this principle, what you refer to as a "lofty ideal," there are places where it is lived out better (which also means there are places where it is not being lived out as well) than in other places.

The reason we do not in the EFCA have a mandate to force pastors or churches to follow a certain course is because of our church polity. That is to say, because of our congregational government, local churches are autonomous. EFC churches are also interdependent, which mandates they adopt our EFCA Statement of Faith. But because of their autonomy, there are things we will not mandate from outside the local church. That is both a strength and a weakness. But it is reflective of the polity of the EFCA.

Chapter 20 Trying to Maintain

As we move into the new year of 2016, I back off on trying to change anything about this church. "Just leave them alone," is Gordon's advice. We are supremely unhappy, but Erin's wedding is not until September and somehow, we need to make it that far. Maybe it is just us. Maybe we just need to put our heads in the sand like most of the other people and follow like sheep. Maybe we are making too big a deal of everything. Gordon and I make the decision to re-engage at a limited level and see how it goes if we are not involved in any leadership positions. We do love the people here and most of our social life has been with people from this church. I agree to count offering money. Gordon agrees to run the sound system. He even agrees to accept a position again on the building committee. Together we sign up for a couple days of nursery duty.

∞∞∞∞

In early May of 2016, Pastor Joshua sends me an e-mail link to an article entitled, "TRUTH, TRUST, and TESTIMONY in a TIME of TENSION: A Statement from the Calvinism Advisory Committee."[27] This is an article written by the Calvinism Advisory Committee of the Southern Baptist Convention in an effort to unite southern Baptists around an issue that is threatening to divide the denomination. "We recognize that significant theological disagreement on such issues has occurred with respect to Calvinism. It is, therefore, our responsibility to come together with open hearts and minds in order to speak truthfully, honestly, and respectfully about these theological and doctrinal issues that concern us, threaten to divide us, and compel us into conversation."[27]

Joshua's comment to me is "I read this today and thought it might be helpful for you to read as well. If the Southern Baptists can work together, perhaps we can too."

After reading it, I am excited. Maybe we are making progress. I respond to him.

I do like the article and think this is what we all need to strive for. I agree with all ten points under truth and recognize the tensions if we are to work together under Christ. Your comment was, "If the Baptists can do it so can we." My only question is, who is "we"? If the "we" is only you and me, then I am afraid that the end result desired will not happen. If the "we" is all the leadership of the church (elders and Pastors) who can commit to "enthusiastically affirming" such a statement, then I think there is hope. That is my only concern.

Just wanted to share a quote of the day by Austin Fischer in his book, **Young Restless No Longer Reformed**, before I close in regard to Calvinism:

You may have the illusion of a will that matters (in Calvinism), but if you pull back the curtain, God's will is the only game in town. Regardless of the passion of the rhetoric you crank out to make sense of it, the fact is that God has already decided whether or not you will follow Jesus, share the gospel, deny yourself, and surrender your kingdom. Your will does not matter – at least not in any sense that we can make sense of.

And yet, you are expected to act as though it does. You're supposed to run on the treadmill and pretend you're running the race of faith. This forces you into the awkward position of seemingly suspending your theology in order to live faithfully – because living faithfully requires living with meaning and living with meaning requires choice. You believe God determines all things, and yet act as though your will is not completely determined.[28]

Pastor Joshua does not reply to my e-mail. I approach him after a Sunday service and ask him again about the "we" in his communication. He admits that he has not shared the article with Pastor Travis or the other elders. He shrugs, "I assume that they could follow it too." I do not know what that means but it says to me that he does not have any intention of following what is being suggested in the article. I am assuming his mentioning it to me was to encourage me to leave them alone. In order for this to have any hope of working and being effective, everyone in the leadership (pastors too) needs to be willing to acknowledge that there are two sides and be open to allowing such.

∞∞∞∞

The updated Building Use Policy that was started in motion in 2012 by Peter when he insisted that it was the job of the elders to review the policy has now been finished and finally passed. It is just in time for our rental of the building for Erin's wedding. She receives a copy of the policy. I cannot believe my eyes when I see what has taken six years to develop. "Deposit amount is $100, to be returned if no facility damages occur... In addition to a cleaning fee of $80, the building usage fee is $200 for members and $400 for non-members and may be reduced or waived at the discretion of church leadership." I can feel anger creeping up my spine. The original purpose of revising the policy was to answer the question, who can and cannot use the building based on the mission of the church and how are we realistically going to ask for compensation from these groups? The desire was that the use of the building be in alignment with the mission and purpose of the church. The true reason for even looking at the policy has been totally lost in the shuffle of positions in the leadership while the policy was continuously designated as a non-priority. All that has been accomplished after six years is to now charge members $280 when before members could use it for free. No leadership is waiving the fee for us even though we have donated thousands of dollars to this church. It is just one more indication of this church moving towards a corporate style of leadership with little emphasis on relationship. I don't know why this leaves me livid, but it does; maybe because I have tried so hard to prevent this from happening – to hold onto the principle of us being a church family, not a professional corporation.

Chapter 21 The Proposal of a Covenant

We have tried to keep a low profile this year and to accept that we can't stop the Calvinism giant from invading and taking over the church. Maybe we can find joy alone in worshipping here with the many people we love if we stay out of any positions of leadership. For a few weeks, this seems to be a successful strategy. Then in July 2016, members and attendees of the congregation receive a letter from the leadership.

Dear Truth Family:

On behalf of the elder team, we are excited to share with you a church covenant that was drafted at our most recent elder retreat for our members to consider. The elders have been prayerfully considering how to develop a greater sense of gospel community in our church body. Our desire is to see the gospel take deeper root in our hearts, our families, and our relationships. One way for us to do this is to strengthen the meaning of membership at Truth through the use of a membership covenant.

Why a church covenant? In the New Covenant with Christ, we not only belong to God, but we also belong to each other. In 1 Corinthians 11, we discover that our New Covenant relationship with God not only creates, but also shapes our relationships with one another. A church covenant outlines what it looks like to live out these relationships while facilitating unity and providing accountability. A church covenant does not add to but summarizes and applies New Testament teaching for a local church.

For our church covenant to be effective, it will require intentionality not only by our members, but especially by our pastors and elders as they lead us. This is why our elder team has recently embraced a shepherding plan. We believe the Lord is calling elders to be more diligent in terms of encouraging, leading, and caring for you in a more personal way. This simply means that every member (and their family) has been assigned to one of our pastors or elders for the purpose of prayer, encouragement, and counsel as needed.

How do we implement a church membership covenant? First, our congregation must prayerfully consider whether to adopt a church covenant. We are sharing the current version of the covenant we have prepared with you now and have scheduled a congregational meeting for Sunday, July 17 following the service. The purpose of this meeting is to provide an opportunity for feedback and conversation prior to a final vote of acceptance on August 14th. Once the covenant is approved, current members will renew their membership by signing the covenant.

We are asking you as a congregation to do two things: 1) Pray for your elder team as we are still growing in our ministry of shepherding. 2) Prayerfully consider the proposed Church Membership Covenant included in this letter. We welcome your input as together we strive to "walk in a manner worthy of the Lord, to please Him in all respects, bearing fruit in every good work, and increasing in the knowledge of God" (Colossians 1:10).

Working with you for your joy,
Pastor Travis, Pastor Joshua, and the elders (3)

This is the final blow that knocks us reeling. A membership covenant? *You have to be kidding me!* At this point, we have totally lost our bearings. I read slowly through the letter and the proposed covenant. "Once the covenant is approved, current members will renew their membership by signing the covenant," I read out loud to Gordon, "What is that supposed to mean? Does that mean we are no longer members if we don't sign it?" That is certainly what it sounds like. How can we sign something that says, "I pledge to joyfully submit to the elder team by welcoming and testing their instruction from the Scriptures, trusting their counsel, following their leadership...?" We already do not believe what they are teaching and do not support the direction they are taking the church.

∞∞∞∞

Just what, Gordon and I ask ourselves, is triggering this sudden need for a covenant? We both come to the same conclusion. Pastor Travis and Pastor Jack received training in "Biblical Counseling" through Faith Biblical Counseling in 2013 and had incorporated it into their pastoral counseling practice by 2014. During 2014, a member of Truth named Sally came to Pastor Travis in regard to her marriage. She was a quiet delightful woman who served on the worship team. Sally and her two children had faithfully attended and participated in the church for a dozen years. However, her husband did not attend with her and many people had known for years that the marriage was not healthy. By 2014, she had made a decision to divorce her husband. Subsequently, she communicated this decision to Pastor Travis. During the course of Biblical Counseling with him, rumor had it, Travis was determined to prevent Sally from divorcing her husband. She was put under discipline and prevented from any further participation on the worship team. It was also communicated to her that she should be refraining from participating in communion. Communion normally is open to anyone, member or not. Of course, Sally left the church. Rumors fly unbridled around the congregation. Why is this happening? Many people believe her treatment to be harsh and unfair. What is confusing is that Truth does not have a policy regarding divorce. Divorced people from other congregations are welcomed with open arms. There are divorced people as members in good standing. There are divorced and remarried people in leadership. "I can't do anything about those," Pastor Travis responds when asked about this. "But I can have an impact on this marriage." He is discouraged and upset when Sally simply leaves the church rather than submit to his discipline. The result of this, it is said, is that Pastor Travis believes there needs to be some kind of agreement in place that people who are under discipline cannot leave the church until the issue is resolved. This, we believe, is the driving force behind the push for a covenant.

(Proposed) TEFC MEMBERSHIP COVENANT   (version 1.0)

I. Having been led by the Spirit of God[1] to receive Jesus Christ as Lord,[2] Savior,[3] and Supreme Treasure[4] of my life, and having been baptized[5] in the name of the Father, Son, and Holy Spirit, I do now in the presence of God and this assembly most solemnly and joyfully enter into covenant[6] with this local bod of believers in Christ.

II. I pledge, therefore, with the help of the Holy Spirit[7] to be devoted to others in love,[8] to graciously resolve conflict,[9] to forgive freely,[10] to lead a life above reproach in the broader community,[11] and to abstain from every freedom that would jeopardize my own or another's faith.[12]

III. I pledge to joyfully labor[13] to advance the mission[14] and vision[15] of this church, engaging in its worship,[16] ordinances,[17] and discipline[18] while contributing towards its ministries,[19] its expenses,[20] the relief of the poor,[21] and the spread of the gospel around the world.[22]

IV. I pledge to cultivate spiritual disciplines in my life: personal Bible intake[23] and prayer,[24] regular worship attendance,[25] godly fellowship,[26] evangelism,[27] and the making of disciples in and outside the home[28].

V. I pledge to joyfully submit to the elder team[29] by welcoming and testing their instruction from the Scriptures,[30] trusting their counsel,[31] following their leadership,[32] and prayerfully electing their successors.[33]

VI. I soberly acknowledge the deceitfulness of sin[34] and humbly welcome biblical accountability,[35] and I pledge to encourage[36] and graciously admonish others[37] unto holiness[38]. Should I persist in violating or neglecting this covenant, I will submit to the process of biblical correction as outlined in Matt 18:15-20.

VII. I affirm that this covenant shall be fulfilled when either the Lord calls me home or calls me to carry out the spirit of this covenant in another like-minded church.

[1] "Our gospel came to you not only in word, but also in power and in the Holy Spirit and with full conviction" (I Thessalonians 4:5a)

[2] "If you confess with your mouth that Jesus is Lord and believe in your heart that God raised him from the dead, you will be saved" (Romans 10:9)

[3] "We have seen and testify that the Father has sent the Son to be the Savior of the world." (1 John 4:14)

[4] "Whoever loves father or mother more than me is not worthy of me, and whoever loves son or daughter more than me is not worthy of me." (Matthew 10:37). "And he said to him, 'You shall love the Lord your God with all your heart and with all your soul and with all your mind. This is the great and first commandment;" (Matthew 22:37) "I count all things to be loss in view of the surpassing value of knowing Christ Jesus my Lord, for whom I have suffered the loss of all things, and count them but rubbish so that I may gain Christ" (Phil 3:8)

[5] "Go therefore and make disciples of all the nations, baptizing them in the name of the Father and the Son and the Holy Spirit" (Matthew 28:19)

[6] "We, though many, are one body in Christ, and *individually members of one another*" (Romans 12:5). "Therefore, having put away falsehood, let each one of you speak the truth with his neighbor, *for we are members one of another*" (Ephesians 4:25)

[7] "If we live by the Spirit, let us also walk by the Spirit" (Galatians 5:25)

[8] "Be devoted to one another in brotherly love" (Romans 12:10). "And all who believed were together and had all things in common. And they were selling their possessions and belongings and distributing the proceeds to all, as any had need" (Acts 2:44-45)

[9] "If you are presenting your offering at the altar, and there remember that your brother has something against you, leave your offering there before the altar and go; first be reconciled to your brother, and then come and present your offering" (Matt. 5:23-24)

[10] "Be kind to one another, tender-hearted, forgiving each other, just as God in Christ also has forgiven you." (Ephesians 4:32)

[11] "Keep your conduct among the Gentiles honorable, so that when they speak against you as evildoers, they may see your good deeds and glorify God on the day of visitation." (1 Peter 2:12)

[12] "Everything is indeed clean, but it is wrong for anyone to make another stumble by what he eats. It is good not to eat meat or drink wine or *do anything* that causes your brother to stumble" (Romans 14:20b-21)

[13] "Therefore, my beloved brethren, be steadfast, immovable, always abounding in the work of the Lord ..." (I Corinthians 15:58)

[14] "Matthew 28:18-20 (see endnote #5) Also, "We exist to glorify God by loving Him with all our heart, delighting in His Work, and declaring His gospel in the power of the Holy Spirit for the transformation of lives in a vital and joyful union with Jesus Christ" (Trinity E-free Mission Statement)

[15] "Loving Jesus with all our heart; living the Word for the transformation of the heart; serving people from the heart" (Trinity Vision Statement)

[16] "And (the disciples) devoted themselves to the apostles' teaching and the fellowship, to the breaking of bread and the prayers" (Acts 2:42)

[17] Baptism (Matthew 28:19) and the Lord's Supper (Luke 22:19)

[18] "If he refuses to listen to them, tell it to the church ..." (Matthew 18:17a)

[19] "As each has received a gift, use it to serve one another, as good stewards of God's varied grace: whoever speaks, as one who speaks oracles of God; whoever serves, as one who serves by the strength that God supplies – in order that in everything God may be glorified through Jesus Christ. To him belong glory and dominion forever and ever. Amen" (1 Peter 4: 10-11)

[20] "The Lord commanded that those who proclaim the gospel should get their living by the gospel." (1 Corinthians 9:14)

[21] "[James and Peter and John] only asked us to remember the poor – the very thing I also was eager to do" (Galatians 2:10)

[22] "Go therefore and make disciples of all the nations ... (Matthew 28:19a)

[23] "Let the word of Christ richly dwell within you ... (Colossians 3:16a)

[24] "Devote yourselves to prayer ... (Colossians 4:2a)

[25] "And let us consider how to stir up one another to love and good works, not neglecting to meet together, as is the habit of some, but encouraging one another, and all the more as you see the Day drawing near" (Hebrews 10:24-25)

[26] "Day by day continuing with one mind in the temple, and breaking bread from house to house, they were taking their meals together with gladness and sincerity of heart, praising God and having favor with all the people ..." (Acts 2: 46-47a)

[27] "And He said to them, 'Go into all the world and preach the gospel to all creation'" (Mark 16:15)

[28] "These words, which I am commanding you today, shall be on your heart. You shall teach them diligently to your sons and shall talk of them when you sit in your house and when you walk by the way and when you lie down and when you rise up" (Deuteronomy 6:6-7)

[29] "Obey your leaders and submit to them, for they keep watch over your souls as those who will give an account. Let them do this with joy and not with grief, for this would be unprofitable for you" (Hebrew 13:17)

[30] "Now these were more noble-minded than those in Thessalonica, for they received the word with great eagerness, examining the Scriptures daily to see whether these things were so" (Acts 17:11)

[31] "Obey your leaders and submit to them, for they keep watch over your souls as those who will give an account ...(Hebrews 13:17a)

[32] "Submit to one another out of reverence for Christ" (Ephesians 5:21)

[33] "This is why I left you in Crete, so that you might ...appoint elders in every town as I directed you – if anyone is above reproach" (Titus 1:5-6a)

[34] "But exhort one another every day, as long as it is called 'today', that none of you may be hardened by the *deceitfulness of sin*" (Hebrews 3:13)

[35] "Confess your sins to one another and pray for one another, that you may be healed" (James 5:16)

[36] "And let us consider how to stir up one another to love and good works ... encouraging one another (Hebrews 10:24-25a)

[37] "Brothers, if anyone is caught in any transgression, you who are spiritual should restore him in a spirit of gentleness" (Galatians 6:1)

[38] "Pursue peace with all men, and the holiness without which no one will see the Lord. See to it that no one comes short of the grace of God; that no root of bitterness springing up causes trouble, and by it many be defiled" (Hebrews 9:14-15)

∞∞∞∞

There are only a couple of weeks until the congregational meeting where this will be discussed. Normally, I do not speak up in public meetings because of fear of how I will be perceived. But this time, I can't keep quiet. I prepare my objections to this step the elders wish to take. I stand with shaking knees and trembling voice. I am determined to take a public position.

I am distressed by the perceived need to keep changing the administrative design of TEFC. The current question is Will incorporating a covenant into the membership requirements actually change men's hearts. I understand this is an attempt by pastors and leadership to instill new life into the church by requiring binding commitments of its members. In my opinion, there is something inherently wrong with needing signed promises in order to carry out the church's ministry? Should this not be a spiritual motivation of the heart under the power and conviction of the Holy Spirit?

One problem with a covenant between an individual person and the local congregation is that these kinds of covenants are not found anywhere in the Bible and such oaths are contrary to scripture. One's spiritual covenant relationship is to be with God, not the body of Christ.

James 5:12 says, "But above all, my brethren, do not swear, either by heaven or by earth or with any other oath; but your yes is to be yes, and your no, no, so that you may not fall under judgment."

God takes covenants very seriously and before we enter into one, we should be certain that we will keep it. I, personally, cannot truthfully say that I can pledge to follow several of the commitments required by the covenant in good conscience. Signing it, therefore, would place me under God's judgement.

Furthermore, Galatians 5:1 says "It is for freedom that Christ has set us free. Stand firm, then, and do not let yourselves be burdened again by a yoke of slavery."

This verse is proceeded by Galatians 4 which is talking about how the Galatian Gentile Christians' desire to be under the law is inconsistent with their gospel liberty. When we become Christians, God places us under the New Covenant, which is a covenant of grace.

Salvation is given to us freely through Jesus Christ by grace so why is it now necessary to sign a contract guaranteeing our works in His Church.

Gordon and I joined this church twenty years ago because it was a church that preached the gospel that Jesus died for all and offered Christian liberty. It did not have a set of rules and regulations. We have faithfully carried out each of the commitments that the leadership now seeks to extract from us thorough a binding covenant. The wording of the letter leaves the impression that if we do not sign this, we are no longer members. I am saddened and dismayed at the attempt to motivate members through this move towards legalism. I am feeling smothered by the leadership's need to stipulate what gospel community looks like and my gut reaction is to run as far away from this church as is possible.

I agree with the sentiment expressed by one blogger on his blog: (and I quote)

"The problem (with a covenant) is that it doesn't prevent (drifting away). It just masks it. Rather, it's more liable to create a culture of trapped phonies in the church – People lying to themselves and others. I believe it creates the kind of fake 'unity' that will further drive people away who have doubts or

differences of opinion with church leadership, so the church is only left with weak yes-men...

At its best, church covenants attempt to bind us into doing what we're supposed to do organically as a body. Normally, it seems to end up with the members bound to the pastor's vision. At its worst, it's a tool of control, manipulation, and spiritual and physical imprisonment." End of quote

In closing, I believe that this type of thing often leads to spiritual abuse and cultism. Even if the current leadership has no malicious intent, it opens the way for leaders to abuse those under their leadership if not now, in the future.

I finish and collapse into my chair exhausted. But I have opened the flood gates and others begin to express their doubts and opposition as well. The one question that hangs in my mind, I finally direct towards Pastor Travis as he sits on a stool at the front of the sanctuary, "If we feel we can't sign this new covenant, are we no longer members?" He pauses, then hems and haws. Finally, he says, "We have the expectation that everyone will sign it when it passes."

Pastor Travis's wife, Susan, has an observation she shares towards the end of the meeting, "I notice mostly women talking today and we as women should be being submissive to our husbands."

What a bunch of baloney. Although, if ½ of the congregation is disregarded that removes ½ of the opposition. I bring up Susan's comment to Pastor Joshua later, "It wasn't about removing the input of women but wondering why more men weren't speaking up (either in favor of or against the covenant.)," he responds.

"The men have learned to not speak up as there is tremendous pressure to agree with the leadership." I shoot back. "As Gordon found out, not agreeing with the leadership leaves you uninvited to participate in it. Someone said to me recently, 'There is a lot of pressure to perform in this church.' Everything needs to be perfect. I could name various examples, but I won't because it doesn't help to point out what Pastor Travis does not want to see – that he is driving people away by insisting on perfection in everything."

"But slandering his legacy without evidence does help?" Joshua scoffs. "Is it perfectionism or faithfulness to the Scriptures? Again, where's the evidence of perfectionism?"

So why do the men not speak up in public meetings? Since Joshua denies that the men are not afraid to disagree with the leadership, I pose this question to my husband. Am I really that out of touch with what I see?

"The men have several reasons for not speaking up. I, personally," states my husband, "do not want to be shot down in front of the church and be told what an idiot I am. There are some personalities that dominate and push their position through no matter what anyone says. Men, as a whole, have a tendency to avoid conflict and so they simply don't say anything in that kind of environment. And there are always those who don't really care."

Just a couple of weeks later, another meeting is held in the overflow room before the service "to gather input into the covenant proposal." To me it seems more like a marketing meeting. Gordon has no interest in getting into a battle he cannot win and does not attend. I am in an uproar and feel I need to speak out against this proposal as we are done at this church if this is the path this church intends to take. A document is handed out to all those who attend. I find it interesting that it addresses and refutes the points that I made in the prior meeting. "Do Churches Need Covenant Documents? Does Truth Need a Covenant

Document? and Is a Covenant Document Legalistic?" So that is why the elder chairman wanted a copy of my presentation.

"We are not being honest with people if we have a list of expectations for members, but we don't tell them what they are," is the statement Pastor Joshua, who leads the meeting, uses to endorse the covenant. He denies that their covenant is legalistic and insists that Truth needs one.

We believe that Truth is much better served with a document clearly summarizing New Testament standards for Christian living within our local body.

Currently, our Membership Agreement contains the following statement alluding to the obligations of both the individual to the church and the church to the individual.

I understand my membership in this body of believers **implies a commitment** to the church. I also understand that the Truth family is committed to **upholding me** in my walk with Christ.

This is significant because it demonstrates that Truth already has a precedent for an unwritten and implied covenant enacted upon acceptance into Truth's membership. Its vagueness remains problematic, however.

For the reasons outlined above, an implied covenant is insufficient because it fails to communicate clearly what we mean when we say we're "commit[ted]" to the church and to "upholding [one] in [one's] walk with Christ." It is unfair to expect new members to be held accountable to an implied code of conduct. A covenant document gives necessary substance behind the verbiage of our Membership Agreement.

174

I do a slow burn. Is it honest and of integrity to not tell the congregation what the pastors and leadership believes in an open forum before expecting members to sign a covenant? This is the central underlying problem for Gordon and me. My hope was that there would be some kind of official statement from the pastors informing the people of the beliefs that have been brought into the church and how this would be handled with those who do not follow the Calvinistic persuasion. It is inherently unfair to ask people to sign a covenant where "we pledge to joyfully submit to the elder team by welcoming and testing their instruction from the Scriptures, trusting their counsel, following their leadership..." when a good percentage of the people do not actually know what the beliefs are and that what the leadership believed at the founding of the church is no longer taught (ie that Jesus death on the cross was to secure salvation for ALL men if they believe).

The need to be submissive to leaders and be accountable to them is also brought up in the meeting as a reason to have a covenant. I am having a huge problem with this. In my mind, something is inherently wrong with leadership that feels the need to invoke power and authority by continually reminding people that they must submit. Leaders like to use Hebrews 13:17 "Obey them that have the rule over you and submit yourselves: for they watch for your souls, as they that must give account, that they may do it with joy, and not with grief: for that is unprofitable for you" as a Biblical support for incorporating power into their positions of authority. "The Bible clearly calls for Christians to submit to church leadership and because of this, we wanted that sentiment expressed in the covenant document," declares Joshua.

According to Lois Gibson on her blog, www.spiritualabuse.org, "This same word that was translated 'obey' in Hebrews 13:17 was also translated agree, assure, believe, have confidence, be confident, make friend, persuade, trust and yield... The 'obedience' suggested is not by submission to authority but by persuasion." To me this makes sense as this is the only verse in the Bible where "obedience" to church leaders is even hinted at.

"Do you not believe in church discipline?" the voice is that of Pastor Travis in the back of the room.

I hesitate while I try formulating an answer that will not totally offend them. I do not believe that keeping everyone in line is the job of the pastors and church leadership. In the early church, there was no such thing as church membership and the Bible never speaks to membership or church covenants. One became a Christian through the work of the Holy Spirit and that person was immediately a member of the body of Christ. Paul, Peter, and other early church leaders did not set themselves up as authorities over others. "That is a loaded question. I guess I believe that the church should respond to obvious blatant sins like adultery and murder, but I don't believe it is the job of the church to police everyone and force right living."

I believe there is a huge danger when I see leaders using the Bible as a tool to fortify their position of authority. Trust me, I have lived this in my life of origin and I have no desire to go back to that kind of authority. Power is a huge corrupting force and the more righteous a man feels the more it seems to have the ability to corrupt. Can there be such a thing as healthy authority that is exercised by church leadership? My answer would be potentially but only with continually seeking the humility and grace of God and I have met few men who could accomplish this.

I am wound up and I write a long e-mail to Joshua incorporating many of my previously expressed thoughts with a few new ones. I end my e-mail: My only covenant is with God and His Son, Jesus. I am not sure I have changed anything by writing this as I feel I am not really heard anyway. And I am sure, no one will cry when we move on to another church. Amanda

Joshua does take the time to respond to many of my points in the three-page e-mail, refuting many of my statements and characterizing me as bringing charges with no substantiation for others. He comes across as arrogant and self-righteous. He ends his communication with a response to my last comment, "Self-pity is unbecoming and not a helpful way to end a discussion that you hope will yield positive change.

I feel defeated and hopeless and am really expecting nothing. "Just to let you know I got your response. I am not expecting positive change, so I think we will end it here. There is too much resistance to actually hear with your heart what I am saying. I did want to say we were one of those who never signed any membership agreement."

I am shocked at the message he fires back at me.

I think I understand what you're saying: you believe there's a Calvinistic conspiracy among the leadership that seeks to grab and abuse power from the membership at Truth.

Having been here for almost two years, I don't see any evidence of this happening. I've done my best to engage your concerns, but as of yet, you haven't given me any verifiable evidence to the contrary. Have there been changes over the years? Undoubtedly. Have they always been changes you've

agreed with? Most certainly not. Does that make them wrong? No. Unless you can provide clear evidence of actions or changes that violate Scripture or our governing documents, your accusations of foul play remain unfounded. Moreover, refusing fellowship over matters of preference makes you guilty of the very thing you're accusing us of: being divisive. I hope you see the very sad irony behind all this.

I want to be sympathetic to your concerns, but you make it very difficult when you don't provide verifiable evidence in support of your claims. It's up to you if you wish to disengage but know that it's a choice you're making. Also know that I harbor no ill will towards you – just genuine concern for what seems to be an embittered soul.

It's too bad too – I was looking forward to a lively Calvinism/Arminianism debate during Sunday School with you next year.

Chapter 22 The Confrontation

I am hurt and angry beyond belief and I lash out before thinking about the wording of my response. I do not recognize this person who is supposed to be a pastor and a leader.

Who are you, Joshua? Is this how a pastor responds to troubled people? Is this what you learned in Biblical conflict resolution. I never said any of that.

Just Let me share with you a view of how you seem to want to deal with conflict:

Joshua: Refuted that point.
Joshua: Refuted that point.
Joshua: You are just totally wrong on that point
Joshua: Stop being a baby
Joshua: Refuted that point
Joshua: You already brought that up before
Joshua: So what is your problem?

I am your elder and I do know something about life. I do not expect to be treated like a lying, ignorant female by a twenty something know-it-all pastor. I have tried to state my case kindly but this deteriorating bunch of baloney you just wrote is uncalled for. If you want me to list all the offences ever done so you have proof, I guess I could, but I don't always get my message across correctly and didn't think that was necessary. Just wondering - if you asked your wife if the above description of your communicating style is correct, what would she say. I can see why she would be having trouble submitting to you.

You have NO understanding of what it is like to have your beliefs turned upside down so that one just wants to give up on all of it. I'm also very sorry, Joshua, that we can't work towards trying to actually understand each other.

I have made a cardinal mistake in responding to someone in the heat of the moment. And in doing so, I have set off the firebomb.

I find it more than a little odd that you're calling my response out of place when you're the only one making personal and character attacks. I don't think you're necessarily lying or ignorant (have I said or suggested otherwise?) but neither have you stated your case. I'm still waiting for verifiable evidence for the accusations you continue to make about the pastors/elders' abuses of power and dishonest theological agenda (is this not a fair summary of your concern?).

I've confronted some of what you said – not out of disrespect but because your statements remain unsubstantiated. How else do you expect your concerns to be addressed when they are either based on misperceptions or unsubstantiated with verifiable evidence?

Since you're now accusing me of wrongdoing and questioning the integrity of my marriage – I've cc'd the elders for them to review the comments I've made.

I realize that I have created a serious rift with Joshua and I find it interesting that he is more offended about my suggestion that his relationship with his wife might not be the model he wishes to project than he is about my discourtesy in regards to his arrogant and know-it-all attitude. However, I recognize that he feels threatened and has called for the support and backup of the leadership team. A part of me knows that I have stepped over the line in how I have addressed my concerns of his style with him and I want to talk it out and apologize. I dial his cell phone number and set up a meeting for later that next morning. "I just need to go over to church and fix this misunderstanding with Joshua," I holler up the stairs to Erin on my way out. I am confident that we can resolve our differences.

Joshua offers me a comfortable chair in his office as he faces me across the space from his desk. He pulls up the e-mail communication on the computer, so he has it handy.

"Do you have any idea what happened?" I begin. My intention is to look at the dynamics of how we have both gotten off track and to apologize for my part with the hopes that he will also see that his way of responding as a pastor also was not appropriate.

"You're the one that called. You go first," He answers.

"I am sorry about how this has turned out. It was not my intent to get into this e-mail rant. I violated my own rule to not respond immediately to offensive comments."

"You attacked my wife and my marriage. Where did you get that my wife doesn't submit to me?"

"She just made a general comment one time after a Bible Study about struggling to be a submissive wife," I reply. "I was not attacking your wife or your marriage. I was just pointing out that your communication style is bound to cause problems in your marriage as well as your ministry."

"Oh yes, you attacked the integrity of my marriage. You said that she is having trouble submitting to me." He insists. "You took information that was confidential and used it against me. You deliberately and maliciously attacked me personally." His voice begins to rise. "I expect that you will go and apologize to her."

I just stare at him. His outrage is out of proportion to what was said. *What is going on here behind the scenes? Is he worried that his wife isn't submitting to him properly?*

"You are mean and nasty. You don't have a communication problem. You have a heart problem. Even decent people don't act like this," the tirade continues.

Ouch! These words of character judgement and personal condemnation are like daggers stabbed deep into my heart. My husband doesn't think I'm mean and nasty. My daughter doesn't think I am mean and nasty. My co-workers don't think I am mean and nasty. "So I suppose you are going to tell me that I am not a Christian too?" I speak the words that my heart has been whispering to me for quite some time. He does not answer the question but moves on to the next pressure point.

"You need to be broken before this is going to get better. You can't do this by yourself."

I am frustrated and confused, "So what do you want from me? Do you want me to lay on the floor and cry? Would that make you feel like I am more repentant?"

"No, but you need Biblical counseling to help you deal with your heart issues."

"Have you read my books (the story of my life)?" I interject. I had given the books to him many months earlier, thinking that they would help him to understand me better.

"No, I know you had some childhood problems but that is no excuse. You are deflecting again."

"It is obvious that you know nothing about me and have no interest in me," I am angry that he thinks he knows what I need but has never made any effort to understand me or get to know me."

"So now it's all about you." His voice has risen until now he is shouting.

I am not impressed with the unprofessional behavior. If this is Biblical Counseling and this is how they plan to hold people accountable, I want no part of it. I have lost all respect for this man as a pastor or counselor.

I look him straight in the eyes. I do not tolerate being yelled at. This is how my father controlled us. "I don't yell at my husband and I don't yell at my daughter but if you want to have a shouting match, we can do that. You keep trying to preach and yell at me. I am done here." I stand up to leave.

"So now you are going to run away," he places the guilt trip on me. But he does lower his voice to a normal level. I have never been one to run away from conflict, so his ploy works. I sit back down.

"I am sorry," I say, "for attacking your marriage and not watching my words closely. But I think there are two sides in the wrong with how we handled this."

"That's all I needed to hear." He responds.

I wait for some sort of an apology from him as well, but none is forthcoming. "How come I am always the one apologizing when there is wrong on both sides?" I ask. He only looks at me and moves on to the next subject of concern.

"That blog you wrote (about Calvinism) is divisive and handing out that book (Young, Restless, No Longer Reformed by Austin Fisher) to people is divisive. You need to stop. You're giving the church a bad name." Joshua instructs me.

We move on to talking more about the covenant.

"You are going to split the church if you continue to push this covenant." I say.

"We're not going to split the church," is his over confident response.

"There are people here that say that they just want to come to church and worship," I inform him.

"That is the problem. We expect people to participate."

"So you are going to draw a line in the sand?" I question. "Those who don't want to sign a covenant will be out?"

Joshua nods, "Yup!"

I bring up some of the issues with the leaders making all the decisions and my observation of the pastors moving into a decision-making role.

"You have now started to include the pastors as part of the 'elder team,'" I point out. "The founding fathers made the constitution to prevent that."

"What is wrong with that? If the practice is preferential, the elders and pastors should be able to make the decisions. Unless what we are doing goes against Biblical principles, we are the leaders and should be able to lead according to our convictions."

I groan inwardly. Outwardly, I shrug and raise my eyebrows. I am dismayed at the stance of this young pastor and the influence he is having on this church.

Pastor Travis, who has joined us at the end of the confrontation in what appears to me to be a "good cop, bad cop" routine is kind and humble. "Help me understand how I am being too perfect?" he encourages.

I remind him of a recent incident, "Gordon was playing a DVD by Tennessee Ernie Ford as pre-service music and you came and told him he needed to turn that music off. It was not appropriate. What is wrong with Tennessee Ernie Ford gospel music?"

"Oh, there were people here that day," he responds, "and Tennessee Ernie Ford is a little dated."

"What about telling Margaret that she could not be part of the worship team anymore because she wasn't good enough?" I continue.

"Well her piano playing skills were a little rusty and we really needed to work on having our worship team present a polished product."

These comments confirm what I have believed but I still find them revealing and concerning. Can he not see what he has just said?

As we prepare to part ways, Travis makes an interesting comment, "There are people in the community saying that we are a cult, but that is not true," he declares. "We are merely following Biblical precepts."

After two hours, I am exhausted and conciliatory. I do, however, refuse to accept their insistence that I receive Biblical counseling from them. I once asked Pastor Travis to help me with my communication and he refused because he had a point to make so I am not about to be forced into this now. In the back of my mind I know that my saying no will preclude me from ever holding any kind of position in this church again. But I am so shocked by the type of confrontation, that I only want to get as far away as possible from this place. I ask myself over and over, *were they really trying to help me or were they just trying to put me in my place?* I know I fail many times but being crushed with judgement and scolding words does not help me to rise above my failures. No one deserves to be treated this way. We are all sinners and in need of repentance and forgiveness over and over. The whole confrontation bordered on spiritual abuse and it scared the crap out of me. I sensed no empathy, no compassion, and no desire to understand me as a person or to be open to what I was attempting to say. I had already been convicted and sentenced before I ever walked through that door.

I, however, have made a silent decision. I refuse to attend a church where a pastor behaves as Joshua has just behaved. It is July 28, 2016.

But there is a problem. Erin's wedding is coming up in early September. How do I deal with this? Emotional turmoil is the order of the day for both Gordon and me. I do not sleep. And when I do, I wake up with panic attacks in the middle of the night. We are both overcome by anxiety and we no longer trust anyone.

Chapter 23 More Covenant Promotion

A few weeks later, another congregational meeting is held during which a TEFC Covenant Commentary is handed out. The vote on acceptance has now been moved to August. We do not attend the meeting but receive a copy of the revised V 2.0 via e-mail. It contains some rather enlightening information of which we were not originally aware. This is the first that we are aware that the covenant vote also includes a provision for requiring baptism of all new members and is proposing to drop the pre-millennial requirement for membership. The document also details much more clearly the Shepherding Plan being implemented. I do not find anything in this document to be comforting.

∞∞∞∞

After many meetings with members privately and corporately, the covenant vote is moved to September, then moved again to the 1st Sunday in December (Budget Congregational Meeting) and then again to the annual meeting at the end of January 2017. In December 2016, a survey is sent out to get a feel for the likelihood of the measure passing. Although we have not been attending, we are still members and I feel I have a right to offer my thoughts.

Although I was not there at the beginning of TEFC, my understanding is that TEFC was birthed as a result of a church split due to teaching that was not Biblical. I am beginning to understand that what is Biblical on many matters is a matter of interpretation. However, this history, I think is significant in understanding that the same dynamic is now going on currently at TEFC and requiring a covenant at TEFC is contributing to instability and loss of trust. TEFC is a Free Church and as part of the Free church has stood for Christian liberty while bonding together under the essentials. "In essentials, Unity. In non-essentials, charity." Truth has moved away from this paradigm towards a more Baptist structure – a hierarchal structure where the leaders decree the final truth beliefs and the final decisions. Is that Biblically wrong? Maybe not but it is not what the founders wanted nor what attracted us to this church.

The leaders have admitted that there is no commandment in scripture to have a covenant. I personally believe a covenant between a church and its members almost always leads to injured people because of abuse of power at some point. Jesus instructions in Mark 10: 42-45 to His disciples were "You know that those who are recognized as rulers of the Gentiles lord it over them; and their great men exercise authority over them. But it is not this way among you, but whoever wishes to become great among you shall be your servant; and whoever wishes to be first among you shall be slave of all. For even the Son of Man did not come to be served, but to serve, and to give His life a ransom for many." Servant leadership supposedly is

a value at TEFC, but I am confused as my understanding looks totally different from what is being promoted and practiced. Servant leadership has been lost in the push to "hold everyone accountable." This may be a very honorable objective but in one's zeal to hold others accountable lies the danger of self-righteousness, judging of others, and abuse of power.

Due to overwhelming opposition, the vote is withdrawn. The covenant is dropped "for now." Instead, people who joined before 2000 are given the latest Membership Agreement to sign. Shortly after this, a member of the congregation calls us to explain that there will not be a covenant. "You can come back now," is his invitation. But we can't even if we wanted to. And we have no desire to do so. We are no longer welcome, and we will always be seen as trouble makers and just a little lower than the more spiritual.

SECOND COVENANT COMMENTARY SENT OUT WITH SECOND VERSION
TEFC COVENANT COMMENTARY

Preface

Over the past two years, the elder team has spent considerable time reflecting and praying about TEFC's membership process and how we might strengthen it in order to better preserve and promote the kind of gospel community described and prescribed in the New Testament. Towards that end, the elder team has identified three key ways we believe Truth can strengthen membership in a manner that is faithful to the Scriptures: 1.) implement a church covenant, 2.) begin requiring baptism for new members, and 3.) discontinue requiring the doctrinal affirmation of premillennialism as a standard for membership.[1]

We recognize that these proposed changes are significant and have already been the source of much conversation about the nature of membership at Truth. It is the desire of the elder team to lead our body in a direction that unites and excites us unto love and good deeds. In the interest of transparency and greater clarity about the proposed covenant document,[2] we believe it is necessary to provide a commentary to better explain each point.

Before doing so, it is important to explain that the purpose of covenants is to make clear the standard that defines a relationship. Relationship is at the heart of any covenant. Like a marriage covenant, church covenants bring people together by clarifying those commitments both parties must agree to in order to formalize their union. These commitments are not pledges of perfect adherence, but declarations of genuine intent to uphold the defining relational standards that the covenant makes plain. Grace is the key component that governs our relationship with God through the gospel and is the foundation for all interpersonal relationships for the Christian. In the same way, grace will govern our covenant commitments as well. In so far

190

as each participant genuinely intends, with the help of the Holy Spirit, to uphold these standards as evidenced by their behavior, the integrity of the covenant will remain intact. For this reason, continued, willful encroachment or neglect constitutes the only ground for covenant violation.

Unlike a marriage covenant, a church covenant is broader in its scope. Broader because it does not simply define the relationship between two people before God, but defines multiple relationships: between fellow members, between the membership and the institution, and between the membership and the leadership, and all of these before God. For this reason, church covenants are more detailed than marriage covenants. These more detailed commitments should both faithfully summarize key Scriptural commands and uniquely apply them to the relationship in question. With these principles in mind, we now turn to our commentary.

---

[1] While premillennialism continues to be an EFCA distinctive and is affirmed by the elder team at Truth, there has been ongoing discussion about whether to keep this point of doctrine binding for all EFCA church members. A number of Free churches have already elected to make this point non-binding for membership.

[2] This document's commentary is based on v. 2.0 of the TEFC Membership Covenant

Commentary

Declaration of intent: Point I introduces the covenant by stating the participant's intent to enter into covenant with Truth's membership. Being born again by the Spirit, being, baptized, and recognizing one's union with Christ and His church are prerequisites for the participant's initiation.

Commitment to love: Point II underscores the necessity of loving others in the Christian life. The greatest commandment is to love God, but just as significant is the imperative to love others (Matt. 22: 36-40).

Believers have a unique obligation to be devoted to one another's wellbeing in the Lord.

a. This includes commitments to conflict-resolution, forgiveness, and upstanding moral conduct inside and outside the church.

i. Members agree to seek to resolve conflict one-on-one first, and then, if necessary, through godly, third-party arbitration (Matt. 18:15-20)

ii. Members agree to abstain from initiating civil lawsuits against one another (I Cor. 6:1-8).

iii. "Above reproach" is a broad phrase that should reflect the moral character of the Christian in both the public and private spheres. This extends but is not limited to the areas of work ethic, sexual purity, honesty, kindness, humility, and honorable speech.

b. Christ has secured many wonderful freedoms for the Christian and all of them are to be enjoyed if received with thanksgiving (I Tim. 4:3). The prerogative to love, however, supersedes our right to enjoy a given freedom. If engaging in a particular freedom would tempt or cause anyone to sin, we choose to temporarily abstain from that freedom (Rom. 14:20b-21)

i. For example: if one Christian enjoys exercising the freedom of consuming alcohol in moderation, he or she is free to do so. If, however, consuming alcohol would tempt this believer to drink in excess, this believer should abstain from exercising that freedom. If a Christian is in the presence of one who would be tempted to sin (by either drinking in excess or violating his or her conscience by drinking any alcohol), this Christian should abstain from exercising that freedom.

ii. No provision is made for those who would seek to limit another's freedom by imposing their own restraint of conscience. For example: a Christian who chooses not to consume alcohol as a matter of conscience (Rom. 14:20a), may not require the same standard of conscience from another Christian who is not conscience-bound from enjoying alcohol (Deut. 12:32; Rev. 22:18)

(III.) Commitment to the local church: Point III applies the biblical concepts of ministry service and generosity to our own church. Paul's charge to church leaders in Ephesians 4 is to "equip the saints for the work of ministry." The work of ministry must be shared by the congregation in order for the church to function faithfully.

a. While the joy of laboring in certain ways for the church is not always immediately felt, joyful service is a biblical maxim worth striving towards. We believe that those who cannot labor joyfully in a ministry should abstain from serving there in order to seek out another area where he or she may happily serve.

b. In addition to service, the Bible also instructs Christians to be generous in financially sustaining the work of the ministry. The Old Testament and a strong church tradition indicate that the saints of God have given at least 10% of their gross income. We recognize that this pattern of generosity should be continued today. The Bible affords measure of freedom for the Christian to determine how and where one wishes to allocate one's tithe so that their giving may be a joyful expression of thanksgiving to the Lord (2 Cor. 9:7-8)[3]

3 Elders are not privileged with any information disclosing how much any individual gives.

(IV.)Commitment to spiritual disciplines: Point IV highlights the Christian's need to continually engage in spiritual disciplines. The Apostle Paul charges Timothy to "train yourself for godliness" (I Tim. 4:7b). there are many activities that help us grow in godliness, the most central of which are contained in point IV of the covenant.

a. Bible intake may take many different forms, but it must be regular and it must include purposeful reflection on God's words. Daily reflection on the Bible in personal devotions is strongly encouraged (Ps. 1:2)

b. Communicating is a central component to any relationship and must also be central to our relationship with the Lord. Thus, speaking with God through prayer is both a divine privilege and a necessary part of the Christian life that should be purposefully cultivated (Rom. 12:12; I Tim. 5:17)

c. Church attendance and godly fellowship are also significant fixtures in the life of a Christian. The Bible commands that we meet together (Heb. 10:25) and follow the pattern of the early church who were "devoted to the apostle's teaching" (Acts 2:42). The number of Sundays a member is to be in attendance is not specified, but members are expected to prioritize weekly worship by making every reasonable effort to attend.

d. The Bible is clear that we need others and others need us. Godly fellowship is about more than being in proximity to other Christians, however. It's the intentional act of mutual giving and receiving for the purposes of exhortation and the spurring up of one another to love and good works (Heb. 3:13; 10:24). The more often we can engage each other in this way, the better equipped we'll be to "hold our original confidence firm to the end." (Heb 3:14)

e. Jesus' final words to "Go therefore and make disciples of all nations" (Matt. 28:19) makes clear at least three points reflected in the covenant:

i. Making disciples is the personal responsibility of every Christian

ii. Making disciples cannot happen without evangelism; thus evangelism too is the responsibility of every believer

iii. Making disciples is to be done with all people: among our family and with others God has placed in our sphere of influence. For this reason, our families place a special priority on parent-child discipleship (Deut. 6:7)

(V.) Commitment to church leadership: Point V captures both the value and authority the New Testament gives to eldership in the local church while also promoting the need for accountability and discernment among its individual members.

a. Heb. 13:17 makes clear that every individual in the church is to obey and submit to the leading body, known at TEFC as the elder team. Individual elders are also required to submit to the elder team.

b. Biblical submission to this team means entrusting them with the roles of teaching God's Word, casting vision for the church, and executing that vision faithfully. It also means deferring to their collective judgment with regard to preferential matters of church business.

c. Equally significant to the functioning of the elder team is the discernment of individuals they shepherd. Just as the Berean Jews were commended for the testing of Paul's instruction, so our elders teach only what accords with and is not contrary to God's Word (Acts 17:11). Individual members are also tasked with the responsibility of electing biblically qualified men to join the elder team. This too protects against errant, oppressive, negligent, or otherwise ungodly leadership.

(VI.)Commitment to accountability: Point VI safeguards the purity of the church by clarifying our susceptibility to sin (1 Cor. 10:12), our need for biblical correction (Heb. 12:7), and our responsibility to restore others who may be caught in transgression (Gal. 6:1).

a.   Sin is deceitful in that it keeps us from seeing our sin for what it is: a treasonous offense to God. It is also deceitful in that it keeps us from seeing how blind we are towards our sin. For that reason, we need other Christians in our life who will hold us accountable and encourage us so that our hearts may not become hardened (Heb. 13:3)

b.   We have the individual responsibility to approach anyone who sins against us by graciously making their offense known to them privately so that they may repent (Matt. 18:15). Should the conflict persist, the offended party should seek godly arbitration (Matt. 18:16)

c.   We have the corporate responsibility to pray for and encourage repentance from individuals under public discipline, and if necessary, disassociate with those who continue in unrepentant sin (Matt. 18:17)

d.   Members agree to abstain from rescinding their membership while in the process of church discipline.

(VII.) Commitment to covenant fulfillment: Point VII describes the two ways that this covenant may be fulfilled:

a.   In death when our faith is made sight and we complete the race set before us.

b.   By upholding these New Testament principles in another church. Any member is free to leave TEFC in good standing[4] so long as they purpose to fulfill the spirit of this covenant in another like-minded church. Simply revoking one's membership in order to avoid our ethical or doctrinal standards does not follow in the spirit of the covenant nor of the New Testament.

Implementation

In order for the covenant to be accepted at TEFC, the membership must vote to affirm it by an 85% majority[5]. Should the covenant be affirmed, the following will be implemented:

1. **Membership Agreement:** A verbiage change in this document will reflect that agreement to TEFC's Membership Covenant be required for membership.

2. **Membership Affirmation:** An 85% favorable vote will make the covenant binding for all current members whose signed Membership Agreement is on file.[6] Any member who objects to the covenant is invited to rescind his or her membership and continue worshiping with us as a non-member.

3. **New Member Affirmation:** Upon acceptance into TEFC, new members will sign the updated Membership Agreement (per our constitution) and affirm the covenant publicly.

4. **Elder Shepherding Plan:** TEFC's Membership Covenant will be used as a basic rubric for assessing individual and corporate spiritual health. As the standard that defines our relationship to the church and others in it, this covenant invites us to continually reflect upon how we, with the help of the Holy Spirit, might increase our resolve to live out these commitments more faithfully. The covenant prompts questions like:

a. How well do you feel you are connecting at Truth?

b. Are there any unresolved conflicts that need addressing?

c. We've noticed you've been absent the last few Sundays, is everything OK?

d. How has your time in the Word been lately?

e. How would you describe your prayer life?

f. Do you think your gifts are being utilized effectively in ministry?

g. Have you been able to follow up with your neighbor about your last spiritual conversation?

h. How can the elder team better pray for and shepherd you and your family in this season?

i. Do you have any concerns you'd like to raise about what's being taught or the direction of our church?

By adopting the covenant, the actual functioning of church life will change very little. This is because these covenant standards have already been in place by implication. The current reading of the Membership Agreement has been ambiguous. As a result, the elders have been diligent in leading Truth with the very same principles now explicitly stated in the proposed membership covenant. In other words, the New Testament principles that have governed what it means to be a member in good standing in the past will continue to do so, but they will now be formalized in the TEFC Membership Covenant. This clarity will benefit new and current members alike by enabling them to grasp the meaning of church membership in a concrete way. It will also aid our elders in assessing the spiritual health of individual members and the church as a whole. Our hope is that this clarity will unite and excite us unto a greater love for God and one another, as we trust in His grace to work in us for His glory through Jesus Christ.

"And it is my prayer that your love may abound more and more, with knowledge and all discernment, so that you may approve what is excellent, and so be pure and blameless for the day of Christ, filled with the fruit of righteousness that comes through Jesus Christ, to the glory and praise of God." (Phil. 1: 9-11)

---

[4] Former members in good standing are welcome to rejoin the membership at any time.

[5] This percentage far exceeds that which is required for constitutional changes and the hiring of pastors. Increasing this percentage ensures church unity as we consider this important change to our membership process.

[6] TEFC does not have records of signed Membership Agreements predating 2000. For legal reasons of informed consent, those members who joined TEFC prior to 2000 will be required to sign an updated Membership Agreement.

Chapter 24 Withdrawing Our Membership

The sun shines brightly as the morning of the wedding dawns – September 3. It is a beautiful, warm day. For Gordon and me, our hearts are heavy. This year, we have lost our church and now we are losing our daughter, or so it seems. But we plaster happy smiles on our faces. My goal for the day is to give my best for our daughter's happiness. She and her fiancé have chosen this church to be married in and the former youth pastor, Pastor Jack, to marry them.

The least we can do is contain our grief and turmoil for one day. We stand in the receiving line after the wedding and hug these people who have been our friends for the last twenty-five years. We thank them for coming and participating in this memorable event for our daughter who grew up here. And then it is over. I look around the church, making sure that everything we have used is replaced in its original place in the same condition. We paid for using this church and for its cleaning, but I feel committed to leave everything as it was.

"You don't need to make sure everything is perfect," Pastor Travis encourages us to go.

I do not answer him. He does not know that this is our final good-bye. Yes, I do need to leave everything in its place.

The rest of 2016 is a time of stumbling around in confusion and sadness. Where do we go to church? Does it even matter? Are we really Christians? Is any of this that we call Christianity true? Maybe it's all made up by a bunch of men? If John Calvin, along with other reformers, were Spirit-filled God-Chosen Christians, why did they find it necessary to torture by burning at the stake, drowning, and chopping off the heads of those who did not believe like them. Is that really the kind of heart God instills in those he has "chosen?"

If what the pastors at Truth (and all true new Calvinists) believe is true, it doesn't matter much what we do. It is all pre-determined anyway. And if it's all pre-determined, there is no point in prayer. Prayer would change nothing. Also, if it's all pre-determined, then why did Jesus die? Is this all just a theatrical act? God could just save those he planned to save without Jesus dying since they can't resist His grace and saving power anyway and the rest can go to hell as planned.

"I wish someone would just tell me if I'm saved or not." Is Gordon's plea. "If I'm not and there is nothing I can do about it, I might just as well go to the bar and drink myself into oblivion."

"Why could God not make the scripture clear enough that there would not be this proliferation of denominations and groups who all preach that their interpretation is the correct one?" is Gordon's next question.

We no longer have any desire to witness to others. What does one tell a non-Christian friend? "Oh, Christ loved many people and died for them so that their sins might be forgiven. You might be one of them. Wouldn't you like to accept him just in case you are one of them?"

And as I do research, I find that many of the new Calvinistic churches also promote authoritarianism, complementarianism, and covenants. The four concepts seem to come as a package promoted by some of the more prominent men of the evangelical world: John Piper, Wayne Grudem, C.J. Mahaney, and Al Mohler to name a few. People seem to be enthralled with the teaching of these men and follow wildly after them. It has become a culture of men worship. I wonder what has happened to studying and following the Bible? Is this the part of the Matthew 24:24 that Jesus is talking about in the last days? "For there shall arise false Christs, and false prophets, and shall shew great signs and wonders; insomuch that, if *it were* possible, they shall deceive the very elect."

I begin to realize too that there are no Calvinists that live like Calvinists. It's totally ironic that pastors that preach God's "sovereignty (defined as divine determinism)" don't rely on him at all. They are so uptight that they can't rest in His faithfulness and trust that He is working in the lives of His followers and the church they pastor. They need to set up a system of "accountability" (authoritarianism) to make sure the people follow the right path (their prescribed path). They want to pass covenants (legalism) to bind people into being dedicated to their church and to God. And they spend time translating scriptures so that they support the practice of not having women contribute their wisdom to the direction of the church. Oh, you say, that is just not true. In 2017, Pastor Travis preaches through the book of I Corinthians. I make a special point to listen to his sermon (and review his notes) on I Corinthians 11. Coming from a Mennonite background, I Corinthians 11 was interpreted literally. Men were not to wear long hair and women were to wear a head covering. And this was followed exactly to the letter of the law. I want to see what Pastor Travis has to say about these issues. I find it somewhat amusing and largely hypocritical that most of the chapter is dismissed as culturally driven and not applicable for today by modern day evangelical Christians with the exception of verse 3: "Now I want you to realize that the head of every man is Christ, and the head of the woman is man, and the head of Christ is God." Pastor Travis uses this verse to support the interpretation that Paul's "reminding us that God being the head of Christ indicates a woman's submission to her husband or **male elders** in the church is not a dishonorable position." Huhhh.... Nowhere in the Bible does it instruct women to be submissive to **male elders** in the church. That tells me volumes about the underlying attitude towards the place of women in this church. I am not just making up the "women are to be seen and not heard" attitude I am sensing.

∞∞∞∞∞

We have no desire to become involved in another church, but we do continue to attend our sermon-based small group. Most of the people attending would not hold to the new beliefs of the leadership and they encourage us to continue to worship with them. It does provide us with a social connection with people we know and love. We have determined to not participate in the discussions (to keep our mouths shut) and to not bring up our beliefs that might differ from what Pastor Travis is preaching. We plan to be invisible as much as possible.

∞∞∞∞∞

For almost six months, I have been seeking the Lord's help while working on a letter of response to Pastor Joshua. I decide in late January of 2017 to visit Pastor Travis, taking along a friend for support. I am hoping that Travis will help me word my concerns appropriately in a letter to Joshua about the interaction we had during our last meeting in July 2016. *Maybe if things go well, he will help me with a face-to-face meeting.* But if I am hoping for empathy and support from the senior pastor, I am not going to get it. He is defensive and instantly defends his associate pastor.

"You may have been offended by the way Joshua communicated to you but there are some grains of truth in what he said," Travis declares. "I would encourage you to read chapter 5 in *The Peacemaker*-the most important chapter in the book. I would also encourage you to read the little book by Nancy Leigh DeMoss, *Surrender.* Her list on evaluating brokenness (vs. pride) in your life can be very helpful in examining your heart as you prepare to deal with others."

As we discuss the issues that have brought us to this point, the tears begin their creep from the corners of my eyes and my body begins to shake with the sobs that erupt from deep within me. I share with Pastor Travis my grief and anguish over the loss of my husband's faith due to his teachings of Calvinism. He sits in his chair unmoving and expressionless, studying my face. He exhibits no empathy and does not seem distressed at all over the despair that envelopes me. I might just as well stuff the tears back inside me. What difference does it make anyway? Finally, he directs a question to me.

"What would you need from us," he inquires, "in order to continue making this your church home?"

"I need two things," I respond, "I need the leadership to take a middle-of-the-road approach to the Calvinism teaching and I need women to have some place for helping to make decisions about the direction of the church. You don't need to have women on the board, but you could have a small group of women that the board consults for input before making men only decisions regarding the direction of the church."

His eyebrows scrunch toward the middle and his head does a short back and forth shake. "That is not going to happen. I would not be able to preach my convictions," he concludes.

"But," I point out, "Pastor Jack was a Calvinist, and no one would have guessed. So you can preach without making it a focus of every sermon." He just looks at me. It is evident that he is not open to compromise.

"Are you ready to remove your membership?" he finally asks.

I hesitate in answering. That is a strange question and I sense his urgency to have us leave. "No," I finally reply. "I don't think this is a decision for me to make and Gordon is not ready to make that decision."

"Well, I am concerned," he stops and hesitates, "that your presence at small group is divisive."

I am hurt but I get the message. They want us gone. We are the problem. Or maybe, I should say, they believe I am the problem. Our twenty-five years of faithful, dedicated service to this church means nothing. A conversation that I have recently had with a happy supportive member of this church comes to mind, "If Travis saw he was proud, he would want to change that right away. He is not as concerned anymore about what people think. He is just leading." It is strange that she is saying exactly the same thing I have been saying for some time but in a different manner, "Travis is no longer concerned with relationship. He is more concerned with having the kind of church he envisions."

As my friend and I stand to leave, Travis gives me a hug, "I'm sorry it turned out this way." Is that an apology? If it is, it is rather sad. Again, I am struck with the emphasis being placed on the importance of the direction that the church leadership wants to follow rather than on any relationship we have ever had.

Gordon and I make a decision to stop going to the small group. We do not want to go where it is obvious that we are not wanted. We are told that the next week, Pastor Travis shows up unannounced at the small group. He has never attended our small group before though he tells the attendees that he is there to "see how things are going." Really!! What a coincidence that his appearance coincides with my discussion with him that week and his concern that our presence is divisive.

By April 2017, it is obvious that this church will never be an option for us again. Instead of doing what so many people do which is simply drift away, we write a letter withdrawing our membership. We feel that this approach is the one of integrity and honesty.

Dear Pastors and Elders:
We are very sorry that we were so hard to deal with. However, it is hard to leave a family one has been a part of for twenty-five years. In hindsight, we should have left quietly when we first realized that our theologies were not the same. We still do not understand how the message of the Bible can be interpreted so many different ways.

Please remove our names from the membership at Truth Evangelical Free Church. Even now, this action causes us sadness, but it seems to be the best and only way.

Thank you very much for all the years we were able to worship faithfully with this church family.

Within two days, I notice that I have been "unfriended" from the church Facebook page. I still consider the people my friends and really want to continue some connection with them. I send a short polite e-mail to Susan, the office assistant and Travis's wife, asking to remain a "friend" on the Facebook page. She does restore my "friendship," but a note soon arrives from Pastor Travis (on behalf of the elders).

Thanks for inquiring about future access to our Truth Facebook group; however, your resignation and inactivity at Truth will preclude access to the Truth Facebook group. Our intent for the Facebook group is to function as a communication link for those who are currently active at Truth and we will continue to make it available to only active members and attendees... We hope you will use personal Facebook connections with friends at Truth to positively encourage and pray for them.

Ouch! What kind of a church restricts access to their Facebook page? This feels like one final slap in the face. What is it that they have to hide that only members and attendees can be "friends?" I thought the purpose of the church was to reach out to people not necessarily already connected to it. Also, those in the Facebook group don't seem to know that it is only for church communication. People post their adventures, their personal needs, and general stuff like any other Facebook user. A sense of utter

Amanda Farmer

shock would be the description of the reaction I am having that church leaders think they are doing God's will by upholding these "very important church guidelines."

I private message one of the elders. I want to know, is this REALLY an elder decision?

"Just wondering. Since the letter Gordon and I received from Travis was signed, 'on behalf of the elders,' I am curious as to whether Travis seriously brought the issue of whether I could remain a friend on the church's Facebook page to the elders for a vote?"

"It was not a voteable item," he responds, "but it was discussed, and we were all in agreement that there was no point in being a member of the group that is for church communication if you are disassociating yourself from that church."

"Maybe it seems logical to you but is it kind and Biblical?" I disagree with his declaration and my hurt shows in my response, "I would beg to differ that the only purpose of the site is to communicate church information. Just read some of the posts. I made a simple request to remain a friend on the church Facebook site. End of story. I have not harassed anyone or written any derogatory comments. Would Jesus unfriend you from his heart? Did Jesus unfriend Zacchaeus who was a tax collector and the worst of sinners? I guess we made the right decision if this is the kind of church Truth is. First, we are told not to come to the small group and Travis shows up to see if we are there and now, a simple request is used to make sure we keep our distance. Enough said."

"I think you are mistaken," Mr. Elder answers, "I know of no one telling you to not come to a small group, but rather questioning your desire to attend a sermon-based small group meeting when you disagree with what is being preached. No one said you did or said anything derogatory. No one said to not come to Truth, no one said not to attend our small group. When you removed yourselves from membership, after nonattendance for many months, that is a disassociation on your part, not ours… We have no desire for you to unfriend anyone or be unfriended by anyone. That is my take on what we discussed anyway."

I am frustrated, angry, and hurt and I speak my thoughts freely. "Yes, Travis did make comments to me personally that indicated he felt our presence at small group was divisive. And how are we to interpret his showing up there the week after he told me that? I know you don't understand any of this at a heart level and that is the problem with having only men in leadership making all the decisions. They are making all decisions based on logic not love and grace. Ask any woman what she would think about being instantly defriended and you will get a different opinion. The fact that something so simply was even brought up at the elder meeting should indicate something to you. I understand we are assigned the blame for leaving Truth but not once did either pastor ever come during those months we were missing with a willingness to work on things. And that was the big push of having the covenant – that the church would not just let people drift away – that we would care about each other. If there is one way to show love to someone that costs the church nothing, don't you think such an action should be reconsidered."

"Amanda, I truly wish you guys were still part of our church family. You are the ones that decided to end that, period."

A part of me understands that this elder has one allegiance and that is to the leadership team – the good old boys club, I call it, and that he probably does not know many of the details of how things have played out for us. I also realize that he, as a man, has no understanding that our being with the group is about long-term deep friendships – about caring about the people. It is not about attending a "sermon-based group" because we want to learn more about beliefs we don't agree with. Most of these people do not agree with the beliefs that trouble us anyway, so it is not a problem.

Maybe, we ARE the ones at fault. I don't know. I ask myself many times what we should have done differently that would have changed the outcome. If I had been more soft-spoken or more diplomatic, would it have made a difference? But I don't come up with any answer that we had any control of except shutting our eyes to what we saw going on around us. I am outspoken and spoke my mind too freely. This was often interpreted as "attacking." We were highly invested in this church. We were the ones invested to the point that pastors loved us, at least initially. We gave them everything they were looking to compel people to commit to through a covenant. But the result of that is we also then felt entitled to have a say in the direction the church was going. And this was my downfall especially. I fought for a church that was Bible-based in my perspective. I fought a losing fight because the men in power had the control and were determined to follow a trend that has taken over much of American evangelicalism. If I don't care, then I don't become upset and maybe that is the way I need to lead my life from here on out- unattached, not caring with a "do whatever you want" attitude. I made the realization one day that we were probably worshipping the church and not the Savior who came to free us from our sin and our bondage.

We are defeated at this point and discouraged in what was once our vibrant faith. We are lost and confused. We have no church home and can't let ourselves get close to anyone else. For over a year, we move around from church to church, mostly attending a large mega-church for the sole purpose of being invisible. No one notices us. No one makes any attempt to get to know us and we like it that way. For myself, I know that I start to not sleep and to have anxiety attacks at night when we get too close to people in a new church. It isn't until July 2018, when my husband offers to help with some VBS decorating in a small church close to our home and then expresses massive anxiety in believing that he has over stepped his boundaries that I realize that we both suffer from a form of Post-Traumatic Stress Disorder (PTSD). Will we ever recover spiritually, emotionally, or physically? I don't know the answer to that question. I only hope our story will provide comfort to others in a similar situation or clarity to someone who is confused by the new trends appearing in their church. And perhaps, there are pastors out there who might recognize how their agendas and directions for a church can destroy the faith of those under them. Lastly, if you as a pastor recognize that the church you are coming into or that you are in does not hold the same beliefs as you, either hold them quietly or seek another church to pastor. It is not your "right" to force upon "your" church those teachings you hold dear just because you are in a position of authority and power even if you are convinced that your interpretation is the only one that aligns with the Bible.

In January 2018, Truth again is not able to find a man willing to take on the position of elder. So now, the church has two elders and two pastors as their "elder team" instead of the four elders the constitution once stipulated. They are one more step closer to being pastor led only.

Epilogue – Final Thoughts

Late in the summer of 2018, I am listening to a Christian radio question and answer show when I sense the Lord speaking to me through one of the questions. In I Kings 13:1-26 there is a story about a prophet.

¹ By the word of the Lord a man of God came from Judah to Bethel, as Jeroboam was standing by the altar to make an offering. ² By the word of the Lord he cried out against the altar: "Altar, altar! This is what the Lord says: 'A son named Josiah will be born to the house of David. On you he will sacrifice the priests of the high places who make offerings here, and human bones will be burned on you.'" ³ That same day the man of God gave a sign: "This is the sign the Lord has declared: The altar will be split apart and the ashes on it will be poured out."

⁴ When King Jeroboam heard what the man of God cried out against the altar at Bethel, he stretched out his hand from the altar and said, "Seize him!" But the hand he stretched out toward the man shriveled up, so that he could not pull it back. ⁵ Also, the altar was split apart and its ashes poured out according to the sign given by the man of God by the word of the Lord.

⁶ Then the king said to the man of God, "Intercede with the Lord your God and pray for me that my hand may be restored." So the man of God interceded with the Lord, and the king's hand was restored and became as it was before.

7 The king said to the man of God, "Come home with me for a meal, and I will give you a gift."

8 But the man of God answered the king, "Even if you were to give me half your possessions, I would not go with you, nor would I eat bread or drink water here. 9 For I was commanded by the word of the Lord: 'You must not eat bread or drink water or return by the way you came.'" 10 So he took another road and did not return by the way he had come to Bethel.

11 Now there was a certain old prophet living in Bethel, whose sons came and told him all that the man of God had done there that day. They also told their father what he had said to the king. 12 Their father asked them, "Which way did he go?" And his sons showed him which road the man of God from Judah had taken. 13 So he said to his sons, "Saddle the donkey for me." And when they had saddled the donkey for him, he mounted it 14 and rode after the man of God. He found him sitting under an oak tree and asked, "Are you the man of God who came from Judah?"

"I am," he replied.

15 So the prophet said to him, "Come home with me and eat."

16 The man of God said, "I cannot turn back and go with you, nor can I eat bread or drink water with you in this place. 17 I have been told by the word of the Lord: 'You must not eat bread or drink water there or return by the way you came.'"

18 The old prophet answered, "I too am a prophet, as you are. And an angel said to me by the word of the Lord: 'Bring him back with you to your house so that he may eat bread and drink water.'" (But he was lying to him.) 19 So the man of God returned with him and ate and drank in his house.

20 While they were sitting at the table, the word of the Lord came to the old prophet who had brought him back. 21 He cried out to the man of God who had come from Judah, "This is what the Lord says: 'You have defied the word of the Lord and have not kept the command the Lord your God gave you. ²²You came back and ate bread and drank water in the place where he told you not to eat or drink. Therefore your body will not be buried in the tomb of your ancestors.'"

²³When the man of God had finished eating and drinking, the prophet who had brought him back saddled his donkey for him. ²⁴As he went on his way, a lion met him on the road and killed him, and his body was left lying on the road, with both the donkey and the lion standing beside it.²⁵Some people who passed by saw the body lying there, with the lion standing beside the body, and they went and reported it in the city where the old prophet lived.

²⁶When the prophet who had brought him back from his journey heard of it, he said, "It is the man of God who defied the word of the Lord. The Lord has given him over to the lion, which has mauled him and killed him, as the word of the Lord had warned him."(NIV)

"Why did God allow the 'Man of God' to be deceived by someone who also claimed to be a prophet of God and as a result of the 'Man of God" listening to the prophet, he was killed?" was the question.

The answer of the Bible teacher was that he believed the lesson of the story is that one should follow the message given to him directly from God and not listen to all the voices that claim they are also servants of God but have a contrary message to the one clearly given. This hits me squarely between the eyes. God has already given a clear message in His Word and we are not to be deceived by all the messages in our world being preached by and written about by popular Bible teachers.

So what are the clear messages of the Bible that pertain to this situation:

1. Jesus died on the cross for all and His saving grace is for all. John 3:16 "For God so loved the world that he gave his one and only Son, that **whoever** believes in him shall not perish but have eternal life."

2. Christ has set us free from the law. The attempt to return to bondage under a covenant between the church and the Christ follower is misguided. Galatians 5:1 "It is for freedom that Christ has set us free. Stand firm, then, and do not let yourselves be burdened again by a yoke of slavery."

3. Jesus taught the equality of all human beings. Galatians 3:28 says, "There is neither Jew nor Gentile, neither slave nor free, nor is there male and female, for you are all one in Christ Jesus." Ephesians 5:21 "Submit to one another out of reverence for Christ" is often left out of the discussion in the push to keep women in their "proper" place.

Lord, help us to cultivate a close relationship with you so that we might hear your message through your Word – so that we might know the Truth and recognize when we are being led astray by other "prophets of God."

Notes

[1] Global Anabaptist Mennonite Encyclopedia Online

[2] Statement of Christian Doctrine and Rules and Discipline, Lancaster Conference of the Mennonite Church, July 17, 1968.

[3] Barry, A.L What about being Lutheran? https://steadfastlutherans.org/images/whatabout/wa_beinglutheran.pdf

[4] https://en.wikipedia.org/wiki/John_Piper_%28theologian%29

[5] http://www.patheos.com/blogs/rogereolson/2014/03/what-attracts-people-into-the-young-restless-reformed-movement/

[6] 1999 Constitution of TEFC, pages 6-8

[7] Truth Annual Meeting Minutes, January 2001

[8] Truth Annual Meeting Minutes, January 2005

[9] https://www.concordiasupply.com/Sunday-School/Gospel-Light-Sunday-School-Give-Me-_Jesus

[10] en.wikipedia.org/wiki/Awana

[11] Forman, Rowland. The Word. Center for Bible Based Training. 2005, page 2 introduction

[12] Forman, Rowland. The Leader. Center for Bible Based Training. 2005, page 1, The Essence of Leadership

[13] Minutes of TEFC Annual Meeting January 2012

[14] Osborne, Larry. Accidental Pharisees: Avoiding Pride, exclusivity, and the other dangers of overzealous faith. Zondervan. 2012. P 17.

[15]https://en.wikipedia.org/wiki/Council_on_Biblical_Manhood_a nd_Womanhoodhttps://en.wikipedia.org/wiki/Council_on_Biblical_ Manhood_and_Womanhood

[16]The Council on Biblical Manhood and Womanhood website: https://cbmw.org/uncategorized/the-danvers-statement/

[17] Thune, Robert and Will Walker. The Gospel Centered Community. New Growth Press. 2013 p 77

[18] 2013 TEFC Constitution, Article V - I Pastor p. 7

[19] Hanson, Collin. Young, Restless, Reformed: A Journalist's Journey with the New Calvinists. Chapter 4 title

[20] Minutes of TEFC Annual Meeting, January 2015

[21] Smelley, Hutson. Deconstructing Calvinism: A Biblical Analysis and Refutation. Xulon Press. 2011

[22] Minutes of TEFC Annual Meeting, January 2016

[23]Vinzant,D.The   Roots   of   Shepherding. http://banner.org.uk/res/shepherding.html

[24] Chrnalogar, Mary Alice. Twisted Scriptures: Breaking Free from Churches that Abuse. Zondervan. Grand Rapids, MI. 1997 pp 30-31

[25] https://www.crossway.org/bibles/esv-study-bible-none-case/

[26] Strand, Greg. Why Do We Adhere to the "Significance of Silence"? EFCA website blog. March 19, 2018.
https://www.efca.org/blog/understanding-scripture/why-do-we-adhere-significance-silence

[27] http://www.sbclife.net/article/2207/truth-trust-and-testimony-in-a-time-of-tension

[28] Fischer, Austin. Young, Restless, No Longer Reformed: Black Holes, Love, and a Journey In and Out of Calvinism. Cascade Books. 2014

Other Resources

Johnson, David & VanVonderen, Jeff. The Subtle Power of Spiritual Abuse: Recognizing and Escaping Spiritual Manipulation and False Spiritual Authority Within The Church. Bethany House Publishers. Minneapolis, MN. 1991

Burks, Ron & Vicki. Damaged Disciples: Casualties of Authoritarian Churches and the Shepherding Movement. Zondervan Publishing. Grand Rapids, MI 1992

Quotes from the Bible are taken from the KJV, NIV, and NASB

CPSIA information can be obtained
at www.ICGtesting.com
Printed in the USA
BVHW030212121118
532881BV00001B/33/P